Deaf Heritage
A Student Text and Workbook

Felicia Mode Alexander
and
Jack R. Gannon

Layout Design by ROSALYN L. GANNON

A Publication of

NATIONAL ASSOCIATION OF THE DEAF
814 Thayer Avenue
Silver Spring, MD 20910

COVER: Bolling Hall, the home of Colonel William Bolling and his family, at Cobbs, Virginia, was the site of the first school for the deaf in the United States. It opened in 1812, but closed shortly afterwards.

© 1984 by Felicia Mode Alexander and Jack R. Gannon
2nd Printing 1988

Published by the National Association of the Deaf, 814 Thayer Avenue, Silver Spring, Maryland 20910.

ISBN 0-913072-66-4

Published 1984

Printed in the United States of America

Dedication

To hearing-impaired students of today and tomorrow. . . . So that they may know and be proud of their unique heritage.

Foreword

Deaf Heritage: Student Text and Workbook

This Student Text and Workbook are the culmination of a joint venture between Felicia Alexander and Jack R. Gannon to provide complete supplementary educational materials to use with *Deaf Heritage*. Jack Gannon is the author of the book *Deaf Heritage* which presented significant highlights of the contributions of deaf Americans to society in the years between the founding of the National Association of the Deaf in 1880 and the Centennial Celebration of the NAD in 1980 at the NAD convention in Cincinnati, Ohio.

The purpose of the Student Text and Workbook is to inform deaf youth of this rich heritage and encourage them to take pride in this significant history and in their deafness. Generally, the book is written for deaf youth who are upperclass students in high school. It is hoped that it will challenge them to enjoy reading *Deaf Heritage* and relate more positively to its contents. Younger deaf students who are highly motivated readers and want to learn more about their deaf heritage may, with some guidance from their teachers or parents, also benefit from this workbook.

I remember vividly the time when I was a youngster growing up in a small town in Iowa with my deaf parents. My mother was constantly encouraging me to read articles about successful deaf adults in *The Silent Worker*, in the *FRAT*, and in news bulletins from my mother's *alma mater*. She also subscribed to other publications for deaf people of the state association and the local deaf community. These reading materials enabled me to be more aware of the capabilities and achievements of deaf adults, thus motivating me to seek greater opportunities in my own life.

The authors, Felicia and Jack, did a remarkable job of designing the workbook so that readers would be encouraged to follow up on their readings with additional readings, research work, and written reports. I firmly believe that when deaf youth are exposed to great deaf Americans who have made numerous contributions to the deaf community and to the larger society, they will be motivated to work harder and achieve goals as high as possible.

As President of the National Association of the Deaf, I am excited to be part of this special venture. Deaf youth of tomorrow are very fortunate that there are many rich opportunities in the world for them to pursue. Deaf youth can become anything they want to be. Nobody is going to tell them "no they cannot do this or that." There is no limit to what they can be. It is deaf people themselves who can make things happen if they buckle down and work hard to become successful.

T. Alan Hurwitz, Ed.D.
President
National Association of the Deaf

Contents

Acknowledgements

This book evolved from *Deaf Heritage*. Acclaimed by many as the "Roots" of the Deaf Community, *Deaf Heritage* was the first book to successfully record a comprehensive history of deaf people. The information presented in *Deaf Heritage* covers all spheres of interest: education, politics, sports, biographical information, organizations, and so on. . . . but all related to deaf people.

When I was teaching deaf teenagers in Massachusetts, they craved materials about deaf individuals. The first time I brought my copy of *Deaf Heritage* into school, they devoured it. It was then that I decided to use the book with my students. I developed materials to supplement it.

I then approached the author of *Deaf Heritage*, Jack Gannon, to show him my materials. He encouraged me to expand my work and develop even more educational materials to accompany *Deaf Heritage*. The result is this edition of *Deaf Heritage: Student Text and Workbook*.

I would like to thank Jack Gannon for his faith in me and for his ongoing support and encouragement throughout the writing of this book.

Without my husband, David, I would have given up long ago. I especially appreciate his tolerance of hastily prepared suppers, dirty dishes, and an apartment scattered with papers, books, and the like.

Special thanks go to Rosalyn Gannon for her creative layout, to Laura-Jean Gilbert for editing my manuscript and putting up with my handwritten inserts and deletions, to Mel Carter, Jr. of the National Association of the Deaf for his enthusiasm for this project and belief in its value, and to the distinguished members of the Advisory Board. This group of professionals in the field of deafness read and critiqued the manuscript. Their input was invaluable. They are:

Taras M. Denis: Special Consultant to the Superintendent, New York School for the Deaf at White Plains and author of numerous publications related to deafness;

Kathleen M. Fries: Coordinator, Special School of the Future Project, St. Mary's School for the Deaf, Buffalo, New York;

Mervin D. Garretson: Special Assistant to the President, Gallaudet College, Washington, D.C., and author of many articles related to deafness;

Leo M. Jacobs: Retired teacher, California School for the Deaf, Berkeley, and author of *A Deaf Adult Speaks Out*;

Nancy Kelly-Jones: Teacher, Atlanta Area School for the Deaf and author of *Signs Everywhere*;

Winfield W. McChord: Executive Director, American School for the Deaf, West Hartford, Connecticut;

Marie Jean Philip: Coordinator, Educational Services, Language Programs, Northeastern University, Boston, Massachusetts.

—*Felicia M. Alexander*

Prologue

(*Deaf Heritage*, pp. xxi–xxiv)

On August 16, 1816 a ship left France. The ship, Mary Augusta, brought two very important *passengers* across the Atlantic Ocean to America. Their names were Laurent Clerc and Thomas Hopkins Gallaudet. Clerc was a deaf man, and Gallaudet was hearing.

The story of Clerc and Gallaudet began in Connecticut when Gallaudet was home on vacation from his studies to become a *minister*. He had a neighbor, Dr. Mason Cogswell, who had a deaf daughter. Her name was Alice. Dr. Cogswell was frustrated because there was no school for Alice. At that time, there were no American schools for deaf children. For this reason, young Alice stayed at home and did not know how to read or write.

When Thomas Gallaudet met Alice, he decided to try something with her. He pointed to his hat, then wrote the word "hat" in the sand. Alice understood and learned her first word. Dr. Cogswell and Thomas Gallaudet were happy to see Alice learning.

Dr. Cogswell asked his friend to go to Europe. He wanted Gallaudet to see some European schools for the deaf. If Gallaudet learned more about teaching deaf children, he could teach deaf American children! Gallaudet liked Cogswell's idea and went first to England.

In England, Gallaudet visited the schools run by the Braidwood family. They were oral schools and did not allow sign language to be used. The Braidwoods did not want to help T. H. Gallaudet, so he did not stay there very long. The next stop on his *journey* was Paris, France.

In Paris, Gallaudet *observed* classes at the National Royal Institute for the Deaf. The teachers were *cooperative*, and he learned a lot from them. One of the teachers was Laurent Clerc. Clerc was very interested in Gallaudet's story about Alice Cogswell. This interest grew into a friendship between the two men. Gallaudet invited Clerc to move to America and help him start a school for the deaf in Connecticut. Clerc accepted the invitation, and they left France.

While travelling aboard the Mary Augusta, Clerc and Gallaudet taught each other. Clerc taught Gallaudet sign language, and Gallaudet taught English to Clerc. Clerc knew French, but English was a new language for him. Gallaudet was learning to sign for the first time, too. By the time the ship *docked* in America, 52 days later, Clerc knew many

Laurent Clerc

money to open their school for deaf children. When enough people had *contributed* money, the school opened. It was named the Connecticut Asylum for the Education and Instruction of Deaf and Dumb Persons and officially opened on April 15, 1817.

Thomas Hopkins Gallaudet, Laurent Clerc, and Mason Cogswell were *pioneers* in deaf education. Their work, nearly 200 years ago, improved life for deaf children in the United States. Their work will never be forgotten.

English words, and Gallaudet had learned *a number of* signs.

When the men arrived in Connecticut, they asked friends to help them. They needed

Alexander Graham Bell Association/The Volta Bureau

Vocabulary

passengers—N—people on board a ship, train or other vehicle; travellers

minister—N—a member of the clergy; a religious leader

journey—N—a very long trip

observed—V—watched carefully

cooperative—ADJ—helpful and supportive

docked—V—landed in a port; anchored

''a number of''—many

contributed—V—donated; gave

pioneers—N—people who start something new or travel to a new place

Chapter 1

The Early Years

(*Deaf Heritage*, pp. 1–63)

Education of Deaf Children
1816–1851

When Laurent Clerc and Thomas Hopkins Gallaudet travelled to America in 1816, they did not know they would become important people. Their trip changed the lives of deaf children and adults in North America. People still remember the two men for their work almost 200 years ago.

In 1816, there were no schools for the deaf in this country. Several people tried to start schools, but all of the schools closed. There were too many problems. The only people to succeed were Clerc and Gallaudet. They opened their school in 1817. It was named the Connecticut *Asylum* for the Education and Instruction of Deaf and Dumb Persons. It was the only school for deaf children in America!

Clerc and Gallaudet did not know what would happen after they opened their school. They worked very hard, and the school did not close. It grew, and many more students enrolled. The new students were from all over the country. The name for the school was changed to the American Asylum. People thought the school would be big enough for all of the deaf children in America. The school is still open today, but the name was changed a third time. Today it is called The American School for the Deaf. It is in West Hartford, Connecticut.

After the Connecticut Asylum for the Education and Instruction of Deaf and Dumb Persons opened, other people also wanted to open schools. They saw Clerc and Gallaudet's success. Deaf children were able to go to school for the first time!

Within five years of the beginning of the Connecticut Asylum, two other schools opened. The New York Institution for the Instruction of the Deaf and Dumb which later became New York School for the Deaf (Fanwood) opened in 1818, and the Pennsylvania Institution opened in Philadelphia in 1820.

The first *state supported* school for the deaf

Connecticut Asylum in 1817

Gallaudet College Archives

was the Kentucky School in Danville. It opened in 1823 and has a *rich history*. One of the first teachers at the Kentucky School was John Jacobs. He was hired as a teacher of the deaf but did not know how to teach! He was also only 18 years old at that time. Thomas Gallaudet suggested that the Kentucky School hire Jacobs because the young man wanted to work with deaf people. John was hired and rode his horse all the way to Connecticut to learn from Gallaudet and Clerc. They taught him how to sign and how to teach deaf students. When he was finished in Connecticut, John went back to Danville and worked for many years at the school for the deaf there. He later became *superintendent*, and his son also worked as a teacher of the deaf at the school.

Thomas Hopkins Gallaudet died in 1851. During his life, he *accomplished* many things. After Clerc and Gallaudet established their school, many others were opened. Before Gallaudet's death, 15 other school programs for deaf children and youth were established! Many of the teachers at those 15 schools used Gallaudet's teaching *methods*. Many had even studied with Gallaudet and were deaf themselves!

Deaf Teachers

Laurent Clerc was the first deaf teacher in North America. He had been a teacher in France before moving to Connecticut. In Paris, he worked at a school for the deaf. That school *employed* other deaf people to teach the deaf students. From Clerc's

Jacobs Hall at Kentucky School for the Deaf

experience, he knew that deaf people could be good teachers.

Laurent Clerc taught at the Connecticut Asylum for the Education and Instruction of Deaf and Dumb Persons. He was a *positive* role model for the students. They were deaf, and he was deaf. They could *identify* with him. As new schools opened, they also hired deaf teachers. Many of Laurent Clerc's former pupils became teachers at schools for deaf children.

The number of deaf teachers increased quickly. By 1850, 36 percent of all teachers of the deaf were deaf people. By 1858, 40.8 per-cent were deaf. Almost half of all teachers in schools for the deaf were deaf!

After 1858, many things changed. The growth of *oralism* had an effect on the hiring of deaf teachers. Oralism is a *philosophy* that does not support the use of deaf teachers or the use of sign language. Since the beginning of oralism in the United States, there have been fewer and fewer deaf teachers. Today, only 13.6 percent of all teachers of the deaf are hearing impaired.

It is also interesting to *consider* the role of black deaf teachers. Deaf teachers are excellent *role models* for deaf children, but what

---

Time Line

1816–1851

before 1816

—No schools for the deaf in North America.

1816—Clerc and Gallaudet travel to America.

1817—Connecticut Asylum for the Education and Instruction of Deaf and Dumb Persons opens on April 15.

1818—New York Institution for the Instruction of the Deaf and Dumb opens.

1819—Laurent Clerc marries Elizabeth Boardman.

1820—Pennsylvania Institution opens in Philadelphia.

1823—Kentucky School for the Deaf opens in Danville.

1825—Central New York Asylum opens in Canajoharie.

1827—Colonel Smith's School opens in Talmadge, Ohio.

1829—Ohio School for the Deaf opens.

1830—Thomas Gallaudet resigns as principal of American Asylum for the Deaf.

—Dr. Cogswell and Alice die a few weeks apart.

1837—St. Joseph's School for the Deaf opens in St. Louis (first Catholic school for the deaf).

1840—Sisters of Loretto at the Foot of the Cross enrolls deaf students in Loretto, Kentucky.

1843—Indiana School for the Deaf opens in Indianapolis.

1845—Tennessee School for the Deaf opens

—North Carolina School for the Deaf opens in Raleigh

1846—South Carolina School for the Deaf opens.

—*The Deaf-Mute* begins publication at North Carolina School for the Deaf

1850—Convention of American Instructors of the Deaf holds its first meeting in New York.

—School for deaf opens in Clarkesville, Arkansas.

1851—Missouri School for the Deaf opens.

—Thomas Hopkins Gallaudet dies.

about black deaf children? They had only white teachers and did not see successful black deaf people. In 1887, the Texas Institute for Deaf, Dumb, and Blind *Colored* Youth opened. The first black deaf teachers were hired by this school. Amanda Johnson and Julius Carrett became role models for their students, and that was why they were hired. The school felt that black deaf teachers would "create *self-respect* and *self-confidence* and serve as an *incentive* for the students to *aspire* to greater achievement." As Laurent Clerc was a role model for his students, Carrett and Johnson were role models for students at their school in Texas.

Vocabulary

employed—V—hired

positive—ADJ—good

identify—V—to feel the way another person feels; to agree with his or her feelings

oralism—N—the belief that deaf children should be taught using speech and speechreading alone without sign language

philosophy—N—idea; belief

consider—V—think about

role models—N—people who set good examples for other people to follow

colored—ADJ—referring to black people

self-respect—N—a feeling of respect for yourself; feeling that you are worthwhile

self-confidence—N—a feeling that you can do something; not being afraid to try

incentive—N—goal; a reason to do something

aspire—V—try or want to succeed

The Civil War Years

The American Civil War was a very sad time for the United States. The people of the country were divided into two sides: The North and The South. Each side had its own army. The southern army was called the Confederate Army, and the northern army was called the Union Army. Many men died for both the North and South.

The schools for the deaf had many problems during the Civil War. There are many stories about that *period* in history.

Some schools for the deaf had to close during the Civil War. The buildings of many were taken over by the Confederate or Union army and *occupied* by soldiers. Virginia, Louisiana, Mississippi, Georgia, Tennessee, Missouri, and Columbia schools for the deaf were all used this way. The Tennessee School even became a hospital and is now a National *Landmark*.

Some schools closed because the teachers joined the war. At the Kentucky School, John Jacobs' son *resigned* to join the Union Army. He died during *battle* and never returned. Teachers at the Tennessee School also resigned, but they joined the Confederate Army.

A sad *incident* took place in North Carolina during the Civil War. A 55-year-old man was out walking one day. He was on his way home when a soldier saw him. The soldier ordered the man to stop. The man was deaf and did not hear the soldier's *command*. The soldier shot the man and killed him.

In southeastern states, every school for the deaf closed except one. The Kentucky School for the Deaf remained open. Its superintendent, John Jacobs, did not allow soldiers to occupy the school. He told officers from both armies what would happen if they moved into the school. He warned the officers that all of the teachers would resign and the soldiers would have to take care of the deaf students. Jacobs convinced both sides, so the

Kentucky School for the Deaf was never occupied by either the Confederate or Union troops!

Farmers near the Kentucky School heard about Jacobs' success. They knew that there were no soldiers at the school for the deaf. The farmers were worried about their animals. They wanted to make sure their *livestock* was safe during the war. There was only one safe place—the Kentucky School for the Deaf! The farmers asked John Jacobs if they could move their animals into the school. He allowed them to put their cows in the basement. Stories tell about soldiers hearing the cows making noise from the basement as they marched past the school. The men thought they could hear speech classes for the deaf. What they heard was mooing cows!

Vocabulary

period—N—time; era
occupied—V—lived in by other people
landmark—N—a famous and historical place or building
resigned—V—quit; left the job
battle—N—war
incident—N—an event; something that happened
command—N—order
livestock—N—farm animals

The Hessian Barracks at the Maryland School for the Deaf

Sign Language Saves A Life

Joshua Davis was 18 years old and lived near Atlanta, Georgia. He was squirrel hunting one day near his parents' *plantation*. The Civil War had not ended yet, and there were many soldiers in the area. While Joshua was out walking, he was suddenly *surrounded* by Union soldiers!

Joshua was deaf, but he knew that the soldiers were shouting at him. Davis pointed to his ears and *gestured* that he was deaf. The soldiers did not believe him. They thought Joshua was a *spy* and trying to fool them. They thought he was really a hearing person.

The men pushed Joshua to a house nearby. The people who lived in the house told the soldiers about Joshua. They said Joshua was their son and that he really was deaf. The soldiers did not believe them and started to look for a rope to hang Joshua, "the spy."

While the soldiers were getting ready to hang their *captive*, a young officer arrived on *horseback*. The soldiers told the officer about the spy who tried to fool them. The officer rode over to Joshua and fingerspelled to him, "Are you deaf?" Joshua signed back to the officer. The officer asked Joshua where he went to school, and Joshua signed back the name of the school.

The officer ordered Joshua's freedom. He told the soldiers to *release* the young deaf man

Laura-Jean Gilbert

and to leave his house. Joshua's family felt so *relieved* and happy that they invited the *enemy* officer to eat dinner with them. The officer accepted the invitation, and during dinner he signed to Joshua. The officer explained that he had a deaf brother in Illinois. His brother taught him to sign.

Joshua Davis later moved to Texas, became a farmer, and raised seven children. Five of his children were deaf, one was hard-of-hearing, and one was hearing. Joshua lived until he was 84, but he always remembered his Civil War experience at age 18.

Vocabulary

plantation—N—a large farm in The South
surrounded—V—to be circled by something; people making a circle around someone
gestured—V—mimed; acted out
spy—N—a person working for the enemy (secretly)
captive—N—a person who is a prisoner
horseback—ADV—riding a horse
release—V—to free a captive
relieved—ADJ—feeling better, without worry or fear
enemy—N—opponent; a person supporting the opposite side

Oral Education in America

In the early years of education of the deaf, most schools did not *emphasize* the teaching of speech. Most people felt that the oral method was *useless* for deaf children, and most schools used Sign Language. One person was *quoted* as saying,

"It is as *absurd* to speak of seeing sound or reading speech, as of hearing color . . . As one who understands several languages will use the one which pleases and *aids* him the most, so will the deaf person use such class of signs as is most satisfactory to him."

The National Deaf-Mute College was founded in 1864. Two months later, a man named Engelsman moved to New York City from Germany. He had been a teacher in Germany and believed in teaching deaf children without signs. Most of his ideas about oral education were popular at that time, and he was able to start a new school in New York City. His school grew quickly. In 1867, it became The New York Institution for the Improved Instruction of Deaf Mutes. It was the first pure oral school for the deaf in the United States.

When Engelsman's school opened, there were only 10 students. Ten years later, there were 110 *pupils*. They needed more room, so the school was moved to Lexington Avenue. The school is still *in existence* and is known as the Lexington School for the Deaf.

In March of 1864, a man named Gardiner Hubbard spoke to the Massachusetts *Legislature*. He asked the *politicians* to help him establish an oral school for the deaf in Massachusetts. Hubbard did not like the methods used at the school in Hartford. The people in Hartford thought that Hubbard was trying to *"accomplish the impossible."* The Massachusetts Legislature did not give Hubbard any money, but they encouraged him to ask other people. The government also suggested that teachers at the American Asylum use oral methods instead of signs. The American Asylum did not change its methods, and it never became a pure oral school.

Hubbard was not satisfied. He wanted to prove that the oral method could work. He decided to set-up a small school for deaf children in Chelmsford, Massachusetts. Several powerful people in Massachusetts offered to help Hubbard. They told him about a *wealthy* man in Northampton, Massachusetts, who wanted to give away $50,000 to open a new school. Hubbard met the man, and his school was given enough money to move to North-ampton. It was named the Clarke School for the Deaf, and the $50,000.00 was used to start this new school. When it was opened, the Clarke School was a pure oral school. It is still open today and is still oral without any use of sign language.

The system supported by Gardiner Hubbard and Engelsman was called "The Natural Method"—using only speech and speech-reading. The National Association of the Deaf and deaf adults called it "The German Method" because Samuel Heinicke had taught this method in Germany.

Many state schools for the deaf changed when oralism became popular. Some added speech teachers, and some even stopped using signs. The first state school to become totally oral was the Pennsylvania School for the Deaf in Mount Airy.

Time-Line
1852—1865

1852—Wisconsin School for the Deaf opens in Delavan.
　　—Louisiana State School for Deaf opens.
　　—Mr. Bartlett's Family School for Young Deaf-Mute Children opens in New York City.
1854—Mississippi School for the Deaf opens in Jackson.
　　—Michigan School for the Deaf opens.
　　—Gallaudet Monument honoring the late T. H. Gallaudet is dedicated in Hartford.
1855—Iowa School for the Deaf opens in Council Bluffs.
1856—Texas School for the Deaf opens in Austin.
　　—J. B. Edwards school opens in Lexington, Georgia.
　　—P. H. Skinner's School opens in Washington, D.C.
　　—P. H. Skinner's School for the Colored Deaf Children opens in Niagara City, New York.
1857—Columbia Institution for the Instruction of Deaf and Dumb and Blind opens in Washington, D.C.
1858—Alabama Institute for the Deaf opens in Talladega.
　　—Laurent Clerc retires.
1859—St. Mary's School for the Deaf opens in Buffalo, New York.
　　—Home for Young Deaf-Mutes opens in New York City.
1860—California School for the Deaf opens in San Francisco.
1861—Kansas School for the Deaf opens in Baldwin.
　　—Minnesota School for the Deaf open in Faribault.
1864—Congress authorizes Board of Directors of the Columbia Institution to grant college degrees.
　　—President Lincoln signed the charter of the College on April 8.
1865—Columbia Institution's college program is renamed National Deaf-Mute College.
　　—John Carlin and others organize the Clerc Literary Society of the Deaf in Philadelphia, Pennsylvania

Vocabulary

emphasize—V—support; encourage the use of

useless—ADJ—could not work; worthless

quoted—V—repeated exactly something another person said or wrote

absurd—ADJ—silly; ridiculous

aids—V—helps

pupils—N—students

"in existence"—operating; being run

legislature—N—state or federal law-making group composed of people elected to do this work

politicians—N—persons working in the government as elected officials

"accomplish the impossible"—do something that most people think cannot be done

wealthy—ADJ—rich

Time Line
1867–1880

1867—Lexington School for the Deaf opens in New York City (first pure oral school in the country).

—Clarke School for the Deaf opens in Northampton, Massachusetts.

1868—Maryland School for the Deaf in Frederick opens.

—Melville Bell lectures in the U.S. about his work teaching speech to deaf people.

—Presbyterian Mission Sabbath School opens as first day school for the deaf (later renamed Pittsburgh School for the Deaf and again renamed Western Pennsylvania School for the Deaf).

1869—Nebraska School for the Deaf opens in Omaha.

—Horace Mann School opens in Boston, Massachusetts.

—North Carolina opens first school for black deaf children in Raleigh, named the Institution for Colored Deaf and Dumb and Blind Children.

—St. Joseph's School for the Deaf opens in New York City.

—Laurent Clerc dies at age 83.

1870—West Virginia School for the Deaf and Blind opens in Romney.

—Oregon School for the Deaf opens in Salem.

1872—Alexander G. Bell opens speech school for teachers of the deaf in Boston.

—Maryland School for the Colored Deaf and Blind opens in Baltimore.

1874—First adult education for the deaf begins in New York City.

—Cincinnati Public School for the Deaf opens.

—Chicago Day Schools for the Deaf open.

1876—St. John's School for the Deaf opens in Wisconsin.

—Alexander G. Bell exhibits his new invention, the telephone.

—New England Industrial School for Deaf-Mutes opens in Beverly, Massachusetts, (later renamed Beverly School).

1877—Knapp School in Baltimore starts accepting deaf students to be in classes with hearing students (first integrated classes).

1878—Gallaudet Day School opens in St. Louis, Missouri.

—First International Congress on Education of the Deaf meets in Paris, France.

1880—National Association of the Deaf is established in Cincinnati, Ohio.

—International Congress on Education of the Deaf meets in Milan, Italy, and passes resolution against the use of sign language to teach deaf children.

Chapter 2

The Late 1800s
(Deaf Heritage, pp. 59–79)

1880: A Year To Remember

By 1880, there were 38 schools for deaf students in America. The *census* recorded 33,000 deaf people in the country, but there were probably even more. There were many state associations of the deaf and new groups starting every day. Many good things had happened for deaf people since 1817, the year that the first permanent school for the deaf opened in Connecticut!

The idea of a national organization for deaf people started in 1850. At that time, a group of deaf people met in Hartford to honor Clerc and Gallaudet. There were only a few deaf leaders; however, people kept thinking about an organization for the deaf. They believed that deaf people needed and wanted that kind of an organization. Finally, a *regional* group was established: the New England Gallaudet Association of the Deaf.

Deaf people wanted their own association for two main reasons. They wanted to help improve the educational system, and they wanted hearing people to know and under-

stand deafness. Deaf people realized that the new oral method would *create* problems for them. They knew they had to protect the children in the schools for the deaf. There were other problems to face, and many deaf people became strong leaders in the late 1800s.

During the summer of 1880, there was a *national* convention for the deaf. It was held in Cincinnati, Ohio. There were people at the convention from 21 different states. Robert McGregor, Edwin A. Hodgson, and Edmund Booth were three deaf people who *emerged* as leaders at the *convention*. Booth was the owner of a newspaper in Iowa. McGregor was the founder and principal of the Cincinnati Day School of the Deaf. Hodgson was editor of the famous newspaper, *Deaf-Mutes Journal*. The convention was a success. McGregor was elected the first president of the new organization established by the convention. It was called the National Association of Deaf-Mutes. Later, the name was changed to the National Association of the Deaf. It is still strong today,

*Robert McGregor, first President of the
National Association of the Deaf*

Gallaudet College Archives

Thus, 1880 was an important year for deaf people. The National Association of the Deaf was born, and deaf leaders started to emerge, but the Milan Congress made a major decision that changed the lives of many deaf children.

over 100 years later!

During the summer of 1880, there was another convention. It was in Milan, Italy. Teachers of the deaf from all over the world *convened* to discuss their ideas at the International Congress of Education of the Deaf. There were five *delegates* from the U.S., and one was Edward M. Gallaudet. He was the youngest son of Thomas H. Gallaudet. Most of the people at the convention were teachers of the deaf, but only one was a deaf teacher. He was an American, James Denison.

The purpose of the convention was to improve the system for educating deaf students. During the meetings, a new idea was presented and voted on. The idea was to have all schools for the deaf use only speech and *speechreading* with no signs. Although the Americans voted against the proposal, many other people supported it; the idea passed. As a result of the Milan convention, sign language was *banned* in most schools for the deaf around the world.

The Influence of Alexander Graham Bell

Alexander Graham Bell invented the telephone and became a very famous man. He also wrote an *article* which he *presented* in 1883. His research paper was about deaf people. He called his article "Upon the *Formation* of a Deaf *Variety* of the Human Race." He presented it to the National Science Academy in New Haven, Connecticut, in 1883.

In his article, Dr. Bell explained why there were so many deaf children. He believed that when deaf adults married each other, they would have deaf children. He thought that this was bad. Dr. Bell blamed the schools for the deaf for causing marriages between deaf people. He did not like the idea of these inter-marriages and tried to think of ways to stop them. He would have preferred that deaf children be taught at hearing schools. He was not a supporter of schools for the deaf. Bell felt that deaf people would not mix with hearing people if they went to separate schools.

Dr. Bell was upset about other things, too. He noticed that deaf people *socialized* with other deaf people. He felt that socializing with other deaf people was bad; deaf people should socialize with hearing people. Bell tried to start a new law that would make it *illegal* for deaf people to marry each other. He gave up this idea when he realized that such a law could not be *enforced*.

Dr. Bell also had strong feelings about edu-cation of deaf children. He wanted deaf chil-dren to be with hearing children in school. He thought that the deaf children could learn normal behavior from the hearing children. Bell was against the use of deaf teachers, too, because he thought this added to the prob-lem of a deaf "race" in America.

Many people criticized Dr. Bell for his views on deaf education and intermarriage. One *critic* was Dr. Phillip Gillett. Dr. Gillett was the superintendent of the Illinois School for the Deaf. He said that most deaf people had hearing parents, and only two percent of his students had deaf parents! He said Bell was wrong about intermarriage.

Vocabulary

article—N—a research paper or story printed in a newspaper or magazine
presented—V—made a speech about his work
formation—N—creation
variety—N—breed
socialized—V—had friendships with; participated in social activities
illegal—ADJ—against the law
enforce—V—make sure people obey a law
critic—N—a person who analyzes or dis-cusses another person, place or thing

Dr. Alexander Graham Bell

Alexander Graham Bell Association/The Volta Bureau

More About Alexander Graham Bell

Alexander Bell was married to a deaf woman named Mabel Hubbard. Her father was the man responsible for establishing the Clarke School for the Deaf. His name was Gardiner Hubbard.

Bell's wife was an oral deaf person. The couple communicated without signs. Dr. Bell knew how to sign, but never used sign lan-guage with his wife.

Many people did not agree with Dr. Bell. A deaf teacher, George Veditz, was afraid that Dr. Bell would *influence* people. He said that deaf people were frightened by Bell because he acted like a friend, but tried to

George W. Veditz

hearing person, he believed that sign language was important. He felt that deaf children needed to be taught with signs. E. M. Gallaudet was also the president of the National Deaf-Mute College and used the "combined system" there. The system Gallaudet *advocated* included both speech and sign language. For many years, Bell and Gallaudet disagreed about deaf education.

Bell had another theory which he never proved. He believed that deaf children who signed would not have good English skills. He could never prove this, and now many people have tried to prove the *opposite*! A lot of new *research* shows that many deaf children whose parents sign (and are deaf) do better schoolwork than deaf children who do not sign at home!

separate them.

Another person who disagreed with Dr. Bell's ideas was Edward Miner Gallaudet. He was the youngest son of Thomas Hopkins Gallaudet. Edward's mother was deaf, and he grew up with his father's students in Connecticut. Although E. M. Gallaudet was a

Vocabulary

influence—V—make someone agree; convince

advocated—V—recommended, encouraged and supported

opposite—ADJ—unlike; reverse

research—N—special investigations

Time Line
1880–1900

1880—National Association of Deaf-Mutes founded in Ohio.

—International Congress on Education of the Deaf passed rule banning sign language in schools for the deaf.

1881—Tennessee School for Colored Deaf and Dumb opens.

1883—The Voice and Hearing School opens in Chicago.

—Pennsylvania Oral School for the Deaf opens in Scranton.

1884—Ephpheta Catholic School for the Deaf opens in Chicago.

—Utah School for the Deaf opens in Ogden.

—Northern New York School for the Deaf opens in Malone.

1885—Maria Consila Deaf-Mute Institution opens in Missouri.

—New Mexico School for the Deaf opens in Santa Fe.

—Florida School for the Deaf opens in St. Augustine.

1886—St. Mary's School for the Deaf opens in St. Paul, Minnesota.

—Evansville School for the Deaf opens in Indiana.

1887—Texas Institute for the Deaf, Dumb and Blind Colored Youth opens near Austin.

—Women admitted to National Deaf-Mute College.

—Home for Little Children Who Cannot Hear opens in Boston.

—A. G. Bell establishes Volta Bureau.

1888—Kindergarten and Primary School for Hearing and Deaf Children opens in Washington, D.C.

—Eastern Iowa School for the Deaf opens in Dubuque.

1889—Albany Home School for the Oral Instruction of the Deaf opens in New York.

—Graduates of the National Deaf-Mute College establish alumni association.

—Thomas Gallaudet is honored by the NAD at the National Deaf-Mute College.

1890—A. G. Bell establishes "American Association to Promote the Teaching of Speech to the Deaf" (now the Alexander Graham Bell Association).

—North Dakota School for the Deaf opens in Devils Lake.

1891—Teacher Training Program opens at National Deaf-Mute College.

1892—Home for the Training in Speech of Deaf Children Before They are of School Age opens in Philadelphia.

1893—Cleveland Day School for the Deaf opens in Ohio.

—World Congress of the Deaf meets in Chicago.

1894—Sara Fuller School is established by parents of deaf children in Medford, Massachusetts.

—National Deaf-Mute College is renamed Gallaudet College.

—Wright-Humason School (Wright Oral School) opens in New York City.

1895—St. Joseph's School for the Deaf opens in California.

—Minneapolis Day School for the Deaf opens in Minnesota.

1897—St. Francis Xavier School for the Deaf opens in Baltimore, Maryland.

1899—Boston School for the Deaf opens in Massachusetts.

Chapter 3

Biographical Information

(Deaf Heritage, pp. 62–78 and pp. 96, 250, and 297)

There have been many deaf people who have done interesting things in the past 200 years. In this chapter, you will read about some *notable* men and women who have influenced the culture and history of deaf people in North America.

Robert P. McGregor
(1849–1926)

Robert P. McGregor went to school at the Ohio School for the Deaf and then Gallaudet College. When the National Association of the Deaf was established in 1880, McGregor was 30 years old. Deaf people respected McGregor because he was such a good *orator* and knew how to communicate his ideas to an audience. He was a writer, too, and always worked to improve life for deaf people. McGregor was elected the first president of the National Association of the Deaf in 1880, and one year later became principal of the Colorado School for the Deaf and Blind. After one year in Colorado, he moved back to Ohio and became principal of his former school, the Ohio School for the Deaf. Robert McGregor retired in 1920 and died in 1926 when he was hit by an automobile.

Edwin A. Hodgson
(1854–1933)

Edwin Allen Hodgson was born in Manchester, England, in 1854. His family moved to America when Hodgson was a child. He was an excellent student and was skilled in French, Greek, and Latin. His plan was to become a lawyer. In 1872, Hodgson's life changed when he became sick with meningitis. The sickness caused him to become deaf.

After he became deaf, Edwin Hodgson decided to learn printing. He thought it was an *artistic* field and not just a *technical* one. In 1876, the New York Institution for the Deaf hired Hodgson to start a printing department at the school.

The same year that Hodgson started working at the New York Institution, the school

Edwin A. Hodgson

damaged one of Booth's eyes and left him with a hearing loss, too. By the time he was eight years old, he was totally deaf.

When he was 17, Edmund Booth enrolled in the American School (Connecticut Asylum) where he studied for several years. One of Booth's teachers was Laurent Clerc. After Booth finished his schooling, he became a teacher and worked at the American School until 1839. At that time, he had a problem with his lungs and had to resign.

Booth left Connecticut and moved to Iowa where he married a former student, Mary Walworth. Booth worked for the Iowa House of Representatives as a clerk. Although he was in an *isolated* part of the country, the midwest, Booth made a strong *contribution* to the deaf community. He attended the first convention of the National Association of the Deaf, at the age of 70, and was even *nominated* for the presidency. He did not accept, however, because he felt that he was too old. Edmund Booth died in 1905 at the age of 95.

bought a newspaper called *The Deaf-Mutes' Journal,* and Hodgson became the editor. Hodgson had many new ideas about the newspaper and believed it could be read all over the country. That newspaper did become powerful, and Hodgson used *The Deaf Mutes' Journal* to encourage a national organization of deaf people.

Hodgson was involved in many activities with deaf people. He was the second president of the National Association of the Deaf. He was actively involved with the Gallaudet Home for the Aged and Infirm Deaf, the Empire State Association of the Deaf, and the Fanwood Quad Club.

Edmund Booth
(1810–1905)

Edmund Booth was also born hearing and became deaf from meningitis. He was four years old when he became ill. The disease

Vocabulary

notable—ADJ—important; interesting

orator—N—speaker; lecturer to an audience

artistic—ADJ—describing something that uses art and beauty

technical—ADJ—mechanical; using machines

isolated—ADJ—alone; separated from other people

contribution—N—donation; gift of time and effort

nominated—V—recommended in a formal way to hold an office

Job Turner
(1820–1903)

Job Turner was born deaf. He *attended* the American School for the Deaf because there was no school for the deaf in his own state, Virginia. One of Turner's teachers was Laurent Clerc.

When Job graduated from the American School, a new school was established in Virginia. The superintendent of the new school was deaf; he was the Rev. Joseph Tyler. Tyler offered Job Turner a teaching position at his school. Job accepted the job and worked for many years at the Virginia School for the Deaf and Blind.

When Turner's wife died, he decided to begin a new career; he became a minister. In 1877, he became the fourth deaf man to become an *Episcopal* minister. After years of religious work, Turner had followers all over the country. He was a very popular, respected, and famous minister. Job died in 1903 and was buried in his hometown of Staunton, Virginia.

James H. Logan (1843–1917)

James Logan became famous after publication of *The Raindrop*. The book was written at the Pittsburgh School for the Deaf in 1910. At first, *The Raindrop* was a magazine printed at the school. It later became a book. When *The Raindrop* was first published, Logan was principal of the school. He and a teacher, George Teegarden, wrote most of the stories. They *created* new stories and made famous stories easier to read. They *adapted* and *simplified Aesop's Fables* and many other literary classics. The magazine was printed *monthly* for one year. At the end of that first year, it was not printed because there was not enough money.

Logan was not ready to give up his special project. He decided to use the stories again and have them put into book form. It was a big *gamble*, but worth the risk. That book, *The Raindrop*, became very popular and is still being read today!

Not many people who read *The Raindrop*

Gallaudet College Archives

James H. Logan

know much about its authors. Both Logan and Teegarden were deaf. Their contribution to deaf children was great, and children still love their stories—100 years later!

Vocabulary

attended—V—went to
Episcopal—ADJ—a Protestant religious denomination
created—V—developed something new; invented
adapted—V—changed
simplified—V—made easier; adapted
monthly—ADV—every month
gamble—N—risk; take a chance on something that could easily fail

John J. Flournoy
(1800–1879)

John Flournoy had an *unusual* dream. He wanted to set up a place where only deaf people would live, and all people would use sign language. He called his idea a "Deaf-Mute *Colony*."

Flournoy felt that the government should give land for this colony, and that the colony would have a *representative* in Congress. He was even willing to *volunteer* to be that representative.

Not many people supported the idea of a deaf colony, and many deaf leaders were against it. One who strongly *opposed* Flournoy was Edmund Booth. He said that most deaf parents have hearing children, so there wouldn't be many people left at the colony after 20 or 30 years.

Flournoy did accomplish some things in his life that were widely respected. He was *instrumental* in establishing the Georgia School for the Deaf. He believed that a national college for the deaf should be opened. *That dream of a college was realized* when the National Deaf-Mute College opened in Washington, D.C.

Gallaudet College Archives

Laura Bridgman

Laura Bridgman
(1829–1889)

Laura Bridgman was born in Hanover, New Hampshire, in 1829. When she was two, she became ill with scarlet fever and lost both her hearing and *vision.*

Bridgman was the first deaf-blind person to be formally educated in the United States. She started her education at the age of eight at the Perkins School for the Blind in Watertown, Massachusetts. Her teacher was Samuel Howe. At the Perkins School, Laura learned the alphabet in less than three days and to fingerspell in two months. She continued to study at Perkins until she was 23. At that time, she moved back to New Hampshire. Her stay in Hanover was *brief*, however, because she was too lonely. She moved back to Perkins and stayed there for the *rest of her life.*

While at Perkins, in 1842, Laura met Charles Dickens. He was a famous author of stories and books that are now classics. He wrote about his visit to Perkins in one of his books.

Vocabulary

unusual—ADJ—different; unique
colony—N—new town or village
representative—N—one person who says what an entire group feels or believes; spokesperson
volunteer—V—offer help in some way without expecting to be paid
opposed—V—disagreed; did not like the idea
instrumental—ADJ—involved; helping to accomplish
"that dream was realized"—the dream became real—it happened

Vocabulary

vision—N—ability to see; eyesight
brief—ADJ—quick; short time
"rest of her life"—until she died; for as long as she lived

Albert Ballin
(1861–?)

Albert Ballin was born hearing and became deaf at the age of three years. He became a famous writer, painter, and actor as an adult. Albert's father, David Ballin, was also deaf and was a skilled *lithographer* and *craftsman.* David moved to America from Germany when he was 22 and became a popular *businessman* in New York.

Albert attended the New York School for the Deaf. David encouraged his son to become a painter. Albert studied painting in France and Italy and won awards for his artwork. His paintings were *exhibited* in New York.

When Albert was in France, he met Alexander G. Bell. They became good friends, and Albert wrote about their friendship in a book called *The Deaf Mute Howls.*

Ballin was a *witty*, interesting, and skillful signer. He taught sign language and wanted to make it a *universal* language. This was one area of disagreement between Bell and Ballin. Ballin felt that deaf children should be taught with signs, and Bell did not agree. Bell was a pure oralist. Ballin believed that Alexander

Bell wasted his energy and money on the oral philosophy. Ballin felt that since Bell could sign well, he should encourage the use of signs. The two men did agree on one thing: *residential schools.* Both felt that residential schools encouraged "deaf *characteristics*."

David Bloch
(1910–   )

David Bloch was born in Germany in 1910. He entered a school for deaf children in Munich when he was five years old. David *transferred* to a technical school when he was older. At the Technical School of the *Porcelain* Industry in Selb, he learned to *decorate* china. He then went to school at the Academy of Applied Art.

In 1938, Bloch was arrested by the *Nazis* and sent to the Dachau *Concentration* Camp. Two years later, he was released from the prison and left Germany. He went to Shanghai, China. He lived in China for nine years and married a Chinese woman. In 1949, the Blochs moved to America.

David Bloch is most famous for his woodcuts and designs on china. He designed a set of china for the White House when Lyndon Johnson was President. His work has been exhibited at Gallaudet College and the National Gallery of Art.

Vocabulary

lithographer—N—printer
craftsman—N—artist; tradesman
businessman—N—a person who owns a
    business or works in a business
exhibited—V—shown in an art show;
    shown in a special place for people to
    look and admire
witty—ADJ—funny, clever
universal—ADJ—world-wide; used all
    over the world
residential school—N—a school where
    children study and live during the
    week and go home on holidays, vaca-
    tions, and/or weekends
characteristics—N—behaviors; traits

"Carrying Wares" Woodcut by David Bloch

Kitty O'Neil
(1946–   )

Kitty O'Neil is a famous deaf woman who is a *stuntswoman*. She is known around the world as "The Deaf *Daredevil*" because her work is so dangerous and difficult.

Kitty became deaf when she was five months old. She was very sick with measles, mumps, smallpox, and fever. Kitty's mother taught her when she was a little girl. Later, Kitty attended public school in Anaheim, California, and graduated from high school in 1963.

When Kitty was a teenager, she was an excellent diver. She won many awards and was chosen for the United States Olympic team. She was on the team in 1964 when the Olympics were in Japan.

In 1970, Kitty set a very important record. She set a *world speed record* as the fastest woman water skier. She travelled 104.85 m.p.h. (miles per hour) on water skis! In 1976, Kitty set other records driving a rocket-powered car. She hit 512.083 m.p.h. and established a new women's record for *land speed*. In 1977 she set more records! Kitty then had a new name: "Fastest Woman on Earth."

As part of her work as a stuntswoman, Kitty has done many very dangerous *stunts.* She has jumped off the top of 10-story buildings. She has crashed cars. She has been set on fire! She has jumped over a 100-foot waterfall and even jumped off a 105-foot cliff. Kitty O'Neil is a brave woman and has earned both of her *nicknames,* "The Deaf Daredevil" and "The Fastest Woman on Earth."

Linwood Smith
(1943–1982)

Linwood Smith died at a young age. He was killed by a drunk driver while crossing a street in Richmond, Virginia. Although he did not have a long life, Linwood Smith accomplished many things.

Linwood Smith

St. Elizabeths Hospital in Washington, D.C. In 1975 and 1976, Smith was a program coordinator at the National Center for Law and the Deaf at Gallaudet College; he then rejoined the staff at St. Elizabeths.

Despite all of his activities and *career moves*, Smith established a *flourishing* career as a writer. He *authored* many articles about the black deaf population in *The Deaf American, Journal of Rehabilitation of the Deaf, Disabled USA,* and *Listening.* He also wrote a book, published in 1974 by the National Association of the Deaf, titled *Silence, Love, and Kids I Know.* In 1983, he co-authored with Ernest Hairston, *Black and Deaf in America* published by TJ Publishers.

It is sad to see such a successful man *perish* at the age of only 39. However, he left a great *legacy* for his *fellow deaf* people by writing articles and books. In addition, he served as a successful role model for black deaf children. They looked up to him because he was successful, black, and deaf.

Linwood graduated from Gallaudet College in 1965. He was a graduate fellow in the Department of English at Howard University the following year. He taught at the North Carolina School for the Deaf in Morganton for five years. Linwood then travelled to the west coast and entered California State University at Northridge. He graduated from their National Leadership Training Program in 1971 and received a Master of Education degree. At that time, he became an administrator at

Vocabulary

career moves—N—moving to new jobs or to a new educational program
flourishing—ADJ—successful and productive
authored—V—wrote
perish—V—die
legacy—N—gift
fellow deaf—ADJ—other deaf people like himself/herself

Chapter 4

The National Fraternal Society of the Deaf

Deaf people are able to protect themselves with insurance today. They can *obtain* car insurance. If they are in an automobile accident, this insurance will pay for the repairs. They can get health insurance to pay hospital bills if there is illness. Deaf people can even get life insurance to help their family if they die, or fire insurance in case their house burns down! Many different kinds of insurance are available to deaf people. Insurance is *accessible* now but wasn't in the past. The reason why deaf people can get insurance today is because of work done in 1898. That was the year when an insurance company for deaf people was born.

In 1898, a small group of young deaf men had a meeting. They were all worried. At that time, deaf people were not allowed to buy insurance. Hearing people had many different kinds of insurance, but deaf people did not. The deaf men were very angry about this situation.

At the meeting, the men elected a president, Peter Hellers, and *officers*. They decided to *research* insurance and report the results at another meeting. For three years, the men looked for information about insurance. They had their next meeting in 1901.

The president and officers worked hard during the three years doing research. They were ready for action at the second meeting. That meeting was *historic* because the men founded the *Fraternal* Society of the Deaf. Peter Hellers became the first Grand President of the new company.

The first few years of the Fraternal Society of the Deaf were difficult. It was run by the men who had attended the 1898 and 1901 meetings. There was no money for an office, so they worked in their homes. Since the company was very young, there was no money to pay for death *benefits*. If a member died, each of the other members gave one dollar to help pay for burial costs.

23

As time passed, the company grew. As it grew, the benefits improved. Health insurance was added. In 1905, the first office opened in Chicago, Illinois. In 1907, the name of the company changed. The new name, still used today, was the National Fraternal Society of the Deaf, NFSD.

Although it was originally established as an insurance company for deaf people, the NFSD has helped deaf people in other ways. In 1904, *The Frat* began. *The Frat* is a newspaper published by the NFSD. It has always been a popular newspaper with deaf people, and many famous deaf authors have written articles for it. The NFSD also has a Hall of Fame. Deaf people who have contributed to the NFSD or to the deaf community are elected to the Hall of Fame. It is a great honor.

The National Fraternal Society of the Deaf is also very *committed* to deaf youth. It has made several important contributions to the young deaf population. One of the programs started by NFSD still exists today. Deaf students who *excel* in school are awarded U.S. Savings Bonds. The NFSD also honors achievement by deaf college students. Winners are given $500.00 *scholarships*.

Most recently, the NFSD joined with the National Association of the Deaf to *fund* a new position. The two organizations each help finance a National Youth Director. The National Youth Director works with the NAD, Junior NAD, and National Association of Hearing Impaired College Students (NAHICS). It is a very important job and will help deaf students all across the nation.

Although the National Fraternal Society of the Deaf started with a small group of men, it has been a success! It is now a very large and a very powerful organization. It has proved that deaf people can work together.

Setting up scholarships and supporting the National Youth Director's position show something else about the NFSD. The company has *faith* in young deaf people. The National Fraternal Society of the Deaf is will-

ing to use its money to help young people. It is providing insurance that the deaf youth of America are good risks and can *succeed*.

Vocabulary

obtain—V—get; purchase

accessible—ADJ—available

officers—N—a group of elected people who run an organization

research—V—to investigate something; to find out everything possible about a topic

historic—ADJ—something that will be remembered for many years

fraternal—ADJ—brotherly

benefits—N—money paid by an insurance company

committed—ADJ—dedicated; ready to help and support

excel—V—work very hard and do well

scholarship—N—a gift of money to help students

fund—V—pay for; support financially

faith—N—a belief that something is good, important, and worthwhile

succeed—V—do well; not fail

Homes for the Aged and Infirm Deaf

Around the *turn of this century*, many people were interested in starting homes for *elderly* deaf people. In 1886, the Gallaudet *Home* for the *Aged* and *Infirm* Deaf opened in New York. It was founded by another son of Thomas H. Gallaudet. This son's name was also Thomas; he was an Episcopal minister. He wanted the home to be a special place for aged deaf people. He hoped it would be a national center for deaf *senior citizens*. Most of the *residents* came from the state of New York, and the home did not gain *national popularity*.

In 1901, the New England Home was established in Everett, Massachusetts. Its *founder* was also an Episcopal minister, and it was supported by the New England Gallaudet Association. In 1929, the home moved to a nearby town. It is still open today and *administered* by a deaf man, Eddy Laird.

In Indiana, some deaf people felt that a home for the elderly was needed. They earned money but did not earn enough to *finance* a home. In 1901, a teacher at the Indiana School for the Deaf helped the group. The teacher, Orson Archibald, wanted to see the home built. He gave a large farm to the group and said they could pay him over many years. Sadly, Archibald died before the home was finished. It opened in 1937.

Another home for elderly deaf people was built in Moultrie, Florida. It was open only a short time, eight years. It was known as the Home for the Aged Deaf and was in operation from 1932–1940. It closed due to lack of funds.

Vocabulary

"turn of this century"—1900; change between 1899–1900
elderly—ADJ—very old
"home"—N—a place where old people live with supervision and help
aged—ADJ—elderly; very old
infirm—ADJ—disabled; ill
senior citizens—N—elderly people
residents—N—people who live in a certain place
"national popularity"—known all over the country; well liked all over the country
founder—N—the person who starts something new
administered—V—operated by; run by
finance—V—pay for; fund

Preserving Sign Language

In the late 1800s, oralism was becoming more and more popular. Deaf people were worried. They were afraid that sign language would be lost and never used again.

The National Association of the Deaf was very *concerned* about the possibility of sign language being lost. The NAD established a *committee* to make sure this did not happen. The committee was called the Motion Picture Committee. The two chairmen who led the committee were Roy J. Stewart and Oscar Regensburg. The committee made many movies of people signing. The idea was to *preserve* sign language on film so it could never be forgotten. Films were made of Dr. Edward M. Gallaudet, George W. Veditz, and many other people. All of the people in the films used sign language.

The films were all made on 35 mm film. That kind of film *deteriorated* very quickly. It was very expensive to change the film to a different size, 16 mm. Unfortunately, the NAD did not use much money to preserve the films. Luckily, the chairman of the committee, Roy J. Stewart did! He saved many of the films on his own. Many films were lost, but because Roy Stewart saved some, they can be seen today. The original films are now copied on videotapes, and many people around the country have seen them!

Vocabulary

concerned—ADJ—worried
committee—N—a group of people working on the same goal or to solve a problem
preserve—V—save
deteriorated—V—broke or fell apart

Nellie Zabel Willhite

Rise Studio

Deaf Pilots

The first *transatlantic* airplane flight was in 1927. Charles Lindbergh flew his small plane all the way across the Atlantic Ocean and became famous. His plane was called "The Spirit of St. Louis," and Lindbergh was nicknamed "Lucky Lindy" after his flight.

Many people became interested in flying after Lucky Lindy's flight. One interested person was Nellie Zabel Willhite. She decided to become a *pilot*, too. Nellie knew she would face two *obstacles:* she was deaf, and she was a woman. At that time, in the 1920s, there were no deaf pilots and not many women pilots. Those obstacles did not stop Nellie because she was *determined* to succeed.

Nellie took flying classes and flew "*solo*" for the first time on January 13, 1928. She became the first woman in her state, South Dakota, to become a pilot. She may have been the first deaf person to fly, too.

After she became a pilot, Nellie's father gave her a plane. She used the plane in air shows and did stunts. She also entered contests and took passengers for rides. She earned money by flying!

In May, 1929, Edward Payne from Ontario, Canada, earned his pilot's license. Since that time, other deaf people have become pilots. The field of *aviation* was opened for them by Nellie Zabel Willhite, a deaf woman!

Vocabulary

transatlantic—ADJ—across the Atlantic Ocean

pilot—N—driver of an airplane

obstacles—N—barriers; problems

determined—ADJ—very interested in one goal; will keep trying until succeeding

solo—ADV—alone

aviation—N—flying airplanes

Time Line
1900–1940

1900—Edith Fitzgerald develops Fitzgerald Key.

1900–1920s—Day schools and classes for the deaf increase.

1901—Fraternal Society of the Deaf established.

1902—Helen Keller earns Bachelor of Arts degree from Radcliffe College with honors.

1905–07—St. Olaf College in Minnesota establishes a department for the deaf.

1908—DePaul Institute for the Deaf opens in Pittsburgh, Pennsylvania.

1909—Virginia State School opens in Hampton, Virginia.

1910—Edward M. Gallaudet retires as president of Gallaudet College, and Dr. Percival Hall becomes the second president.

1911—Arizona School for the Deaf and Blind opens.

1912—Archbishop Ryan Memorial Institute for the Deaf opens in Philadelphia, Pennsylvania.

—Teacher training program at Gallaudet College renamed Department of Articulation and Normal Instruction.

1914—Central Institute for the Deaf opens in St. Louis, Missouri.

1915—St. Rita School for the Deaf opens in Wisconsin.

1917—Edward Miner Gallaudet dies.

1921—Earl Hanson patents the first vacuum tube hearing aid.

1922—Alexander Graham Bell dies.

1926—Edith Fitzgerald publishes *Straight Language for the Deaf.*

1930—U.S. Bureau of Census conducts census of deaf people.

1931—Convention of Executives of American Schools for the Deaf establishes teacher certification for teachers of the deaf.

1934—Federal survey of the deaf and hard of hearing begins under U.S. Office of Education.

—New Jersey School hosts International Congress on the Education of the Deaf.

1937—Ernest Marshall produces a signed movie for the deaf.

1940—Helmer Myklebust publishes *The Psychology of Deafness.*

—P.S. 47 in New York City (junior high school deaf students) opens.

Chapter 5

1940–1960

(*Deaf Heritage*, pp. 219–236 and 255–270)

The Attack on Pearl Harbor

Bill Sugiyama was an eight year old boy in 1941. He was a student at the Diamond Head School for the Deaf on the island of Oahu in Hawaii. On December 7, 1941, Bill was sitting in his dormitory room reading *Life* magazine. Suddenly, he started feeling vibrations. He thought his friends were *fooling around* and making noise. What he felt was not his friends. It was the bombing of Pearl Harbor by the Japanese Imperial Air Force! The harbor was 10 miles away, but Bill could feel the vibrations caused by the bombs. That afternoon, the principal of the school told the older boys to help protect the buildings. They put tables around the *porches* and covered them with *mattresses*. These areas became bomb *shelters* until underground shelters could be dug. That night, the students could see the fires at Pearl Harbor.

After the attack, life changed for the deaf students. Nightly blackouts began. The blackouts prevented the Japanese from seeing buildings in case they wanted to bomb Hawaii again. The windows were covered up, and all lights were kept off. The food supply was also changed after the attack. Food was strictly controlled by *rationing*; people could only buy small amounts of food. Drinking water had to be boiled in case it was not safe to drink, and gas masks were brought everywhere. Everyone was afraid that there would be another attack.

The Diamond Head School for the Deaf was closed until February. The children who lived nearby went home. The students who came from other islands near Oahu stayed at school and did *odd jobs*.

Vocabulary

"fooling around"—V—playing; rough housing

porches—N—part of a house where people can sit outside

mattresses—N—the top part of a bed

shelters—N—a place that is protected and safe

rationing—N—a plan to make sure there is enough food for everyone by limiting each person's food

odd jobs—N—small jobs that need to be done

The clubmobile on the right was donated to the American Armed Services by the National Association of the Deaf.

Joining Up

December 7, 1941 was a very important day in American history. The attack on Pearl Harbor led the United States into World War II. As the attack was going on, Gallaudet College students followed the action on the radio. An interpreter signed everything that was said on the radio, and the deaf people learned with other Americans about the new war.

Thousands of American people wanted to help their country. They enlisted in the Army and Navy and other branches of the Armed Services. Deaf people also wanted to help the United States but didn't know what they could do. Four students at Gallaudet College decided to enlist, too. Of those four young men, two were drafted. Archie Stack became an *intelligence clerk;* Wayne Schlieff was with the Mortar Division stationed at Camp Breckinridge, Kentucky.

Doing One's Share

As the war continued, everyone wanted to help. School children collected *grease, scrap iron,* and *rubber* to help

the army. They also saved their coins to buy *Victory Stamps.* Deaf children at the Virginia School for the Deaf and Blind did their share for their country. They sold over $3,200 worth of stamps and bonds and collected 4,500 pounds of scrap iron and 5,000 pounds of paper! Boy Scouts had *paper drives.* Girls at the Maryland School for the Deaf made 18,000 surgical bandages for the Red Cross. Deaf ladies in Washington, D.C., organized a group called "Silent Service Unit of the American Red Cross." Their organization of women sewed and knitted for the *Armed Forces.*

The National Association of the Deaf bought $5,300 worth of Defense Bonds; the Louisiana Athletic Association of the Deaf bought $1,500 worth; and the Boys' Athletic Association of the California School for the Deaf purchased $1,000 worth of the bonds as did the Minnesota Association of the Deaf. The Washington State Association of the Deaf bought $4,500 worth of Defense Bonds! People all over the United States took money out of their bank accounts and invested in bonds to help America.

When one deaf couple in Virginia heard that there was not enough copper, they turned in 44 pounds of copper pennies! There were

6,192 of the one-cent coins, and they carried them in four boxes!

Not all of the *reactions* to the war were positive. Some of the reactions were bad. In western parts of the U.S., people became very suspicious of anyone who looked *Asian*. People were afraid of Japanese attacks and became frightened of anyone who looked as if they might be Japanese or have Japanese relatives. Many of these people who looked like they were Japanese had been born in America and were United States citizens. As a result of the *suspicions* and fears about Japanese people, anyone who had Japanese relatives was "relocated." They were sent to Relocation Camps until the war ended. The people in the Relocation Camps lost everything when they were forced to move: their homes, their cars, everything! In Oregon, deaf students from families of Japanese *origin* suf-

fered. They were not allowed to go to the school for the deaf. Many persons who had Japanese *ancestors* suffered during the war years.

U.S.S. Thomas Hopkins Gallaudet

The *U.S.S. Thomas Hopkins Gallaudet*

On October 21, 1943, California Shipbuilding Corporation started to build a ship. The ship was built for the U.S. *Maritime* Commission to be used during World War II.

The ship was finished one month later, on November 13, 1943, and named the *Thomas Hopkins Gallaudet*. That same day, the ship was *delivered* to the Soviet Union. The United States had a special *treaty* with the U.S.S.R. As part of that treaty, called the Lend-Lease Act, the new ship was loaned to the Soviet Union.

After the ship was taken to the U.S.S.R., its name was changed to Maikop. The Maikop was used by the Soviet Union *throughout* World War II. At the end of the war, it was returned to the United States. The original name was *restored—Thomas Hopkins Gallaudet*.

Vocabulary

intelligence clerk—N—a person who works with confidential, secret information

grease, scrap iron, and rubber—N—waste materials that could be reused to help build weapons

Victory Stamps—N—stamps sold by the U.S. government during the war to show support for the U.S. government and military

paper drives—N—paper collections

Armed Forces—N—all branches of the military: army, navy, air force, marines

reactions—N—responses

Asian—ADJ—from a country in Asia (Japan, China, Korea, etc.)

suspicions—N—fears and nervousness about another person's behavior

origin—N—beginnings; ancestry

ancestors—N—relatives from previous years: parents, grandparents

The *Gallaudet* sailed for six more months after it returned to the U.S. Later it was sold. The new owners, Traders Steamship Company, named it Amberstar. It was bought and sold three more times before 1955 and had three new names: *Elmira, Pontos,* and *Samuel S.* In 1955 it was *converted* to a *cargo* ship in Scotland.

The ship was bought and sold by several companies in Greece and Liberia. In 1969, the Samuel S. was on its way from Guam to Pusan, South Korea. It *ran aground*, then broke in two, and sank.

The *Thomas Hopkins Gallaudet* sailed all over the world in its 35 years at sea.

Vocabulary

maritime—ADJ—connected with the sea or related to shipping or service on the ocean
delivered—V—brought
treaty—N—an agreement signed by two or more countries; a pact
throughout—ADV—from beginning to end
restored—V—back to the original; returned
converted—V—rebuilt and changed
cargo—N—things to be delivered; material carried from one place to another in a ship
ran aground—V—got stuck on the bottom of the ocean; stuck in shallow water

---

The Post-War Years

After World War II ended, during the *post-war* years, many things happened in the United States that *affected* deaf people.

In the late 1940s the number of deaf teachers of the deaf was very small. Thirteen residential schools did not have any deaf teachers. At 119 day schools, there were no deaf teachers; out of 549 teachers in day schools for the deaf, there was not one deaf teacher!

In 1947, the Ohio School for the Deaf had the highest number of deaf teachers. They had 18. *Tied* for second were the Arkansas School for the Deaf and the North Carolina School for the Deaf at Raleigh. Each had 16 deaf teachers. Third place was also a tie; the Indiana School and the Kentucky School had 15 deaf teachers each. Fourth place was a three-way-tie: the South Dakota, Iowa, and Tennessee Schools for the Deaf each had 14 deaf teachers.

Shortly after the end of the war, the Mississippi Association of the Deaf was successful in helping deaf school children. The association was able to get three laws changed. The state laws were about education of the deaf in Mississippi, and the state association of the deaf wanted to improve those laws. One of the new laws was about teachers learning to sign. The new law said deaf students who did not *progress* well in oral classes had to be taught using signs. The teacher was required to become skilled in using the *manual alphabet*.

Vocabulary

post-war—ADJ—after the war
affected—V—influenced
tied—V—equal; a draw (tie)
shortly—ADV—soon
progress—V—improve
manual alphabet—N—fingerspelling alphabet

Toward a Greater Gallaudet

In the early 1940s, Gallaudet College was a small *liberal arts* college. It *existed* quietly on a large piece of land in Washington,

D.C. After the war, the *federal* government decided to spend $7,500 to study Gallaudet College. The government hired Dr. Harry Best to do the study. Dr. Best was a hearing person and professor of Sociology at the University of Kentucky. He had also taught deaf children. Dr. Best was the author of *Deafness and the Deaf in the United States*. Dr. Best was considered an *authority* on deafness.

In 1945, Leonard M. Elstad became president of Gallaudet College. At that time, the college had 157 students and 24 teachers. Some people criticized Gallaudet College and said it was too much like a high school. When Dr. Best's study began, *rumors* started at the college. There was talk of *expansion*. There was even talk about moving the college somewhere else.

In 1947, President Elstad told the *alumni* at a 20th reunion that: "We want every young man and woman who can profit from a college education to have an opportunity here. If that means 100 new students each year that is fine."

Within 15 years, Dr. Elstad's prediction had come true. Gallaudet's student size had doubled and by 1970 had grown to over 1,000! The expansion was not just a rumor.

The Best Survey

Dr. Best began his survey in 1946. He found that only one-fifth of one percent (.002) of the deaf population was attending college. Best felt that if Gallaudet College improved, then more deaf students would go to college. He suggested that Gallaudet add several departments. He recommended a second preparatory year for students from schools that stopped at the tenth grade. Many other ideas were suggested. Dr. Best recommended higher salaries for teachers. He suggested setting up research at Gallaudet to *investigate* questions about deafness. He saw a need to train deaf teachers because there were no deaf people in the other teacher training programs.

All of Dr. Best's ideas were new. Some people thought the ideas were great, and others did not. Some believed that all of the new plans could make Gallaudet the "Educational *Mecca* of the Deaf World." Others were disappointed with Dr. Best's work and wanted to know more about how to teach deaf students.

Dr. Best's research work did not answer all of the questions people asked. For this reason, the government hired another man to research how to improve Gallaudet College. His name was Dr. Buell Gallagher. At the end of his study, he suggested that the government make a choice: either spend enough money to improve the college or close it.

Best's study received a lot of *publicity*. It was printed in the *Gallaudet Alumni Bulletin* and *The Cavalier*. Gallagher's report did not get as much attention. Many people were angry that Gallagher's report was *ignored*. They thought it was very *significant*. Today, many people believe that the changes in Gallaudet College happened because of Gallagher's research.

In September 1950, 70 new students were admitted to Gallaudet College. This was the highest number of new students ever. Six of them were from other countries: Israel, Sweden, China, Trans-Jordan, Canada, and Denmark. A year later, Boyce R. Williams was elected to the college Board of Directors. He was the first alumni representative to the Board.

In 1954, the U.S. Congress passed a bill that officially changed the name of Gallaudet College. This law made the Columbia Institution for the Deaf the old name. The new name became Gallaudet College.

If there had been no research by Best and Gallagher, it is possible that life would be very different for deaf people in America today. It would be most different for college students who also happen to be deaf!

Newsday, The Long Island Newspaper

Emerson Romero working on a captioned film in his workshop.

Captioned Films for the Deaf

Around 1947, a man in New York bought some films and began adding *captions* to the movies. The man was Emerson Romero, and he was deaf.

To caption his films, Romero cut the films and added captions between the scenes. This was how the old silent movies were captioned. Romero rented his *subtitled* films to schools for the deaf, churches, and clubs, and they became very popular.

Romero's method of captioning had one *drawback*, and it was a serious one. By cutting the film, *"splicing"* it, the *dialogue* was sometimes cut, too. Also, the cost of making the captioned films was too high for one person. Although Emerson Romero did not work for the government, his idea later led to federal funding of captioning.

In 1950, Dr. Boatner, superintendent of the American School for the Deaf, visited the Lexington School for the Deaf. He observed a young teacher trying to make his own captions on a *transparency*. This gave Dr. Boatner an idea which he discussed with his friend Dr. O'Connor, of the Lexington School. They got a *grant* from the Junior League in Hartford and established a new organization. The organization was named Captioned Films for the Deaf.

Next, Dr. Boatner asked a deaf teacher at the American School to help. His name was J. Pierre Rakow, and he was also interested and volunteered to study different ways to caption films. The men *eventually* captioned 30 films.

Boatner soon realized, like Romero, that it was very expensive to buy the films and caption them. He believed that the only solution was a government-sponsored program. He asked a United States Senator, William Purcell, to sponsor a *bill* in Congress. The Senator agreed, and on September 2, 1958, a bill was passed. That bill, Public Law 85-905, established Captioned Films for the Deaf and paid for the loan fees of films. The captioned films were loaned to deaf people *free of charge*.

The federal captioning project was funded by the Secretary of Health, Education, and

Welfare and run by the U.S. Office of Education. By 1970, Captioned Films for the Deaf was spending $3 million on films and other *media* for deaf people!

Vocabulary

captions—N—written words that show what people say in a film
subtitled—ADJ—captioned
drawback—N—problem
splicing—V—cutting, adding or removing a part then putting the film or tape back together
dialogue—N—conversation between two people
transparency—N—a piece of plastic that you can see through; a slide
grant—N—money given for research; scholarship for research
eventually—ADV—later; after a while
bill—N—a new law
free of charge—no charge; without a fee
media—N—news vehicles: television, radio, newspapers, magazines, videotapes

Time-Line
1940–1960

1941–1945—Deaf people make outstanding contributions to America during World War II.
1942—John Tracy Clinic opens in Los Angeles.
1943—Dr. Harry Best's book *Deafness and the Deaf in the United States* appears.
1945—American Athletic Association for the Deaf is organized by deaf sportsmen.
  —Dr. Leonard Elstad becomes third President of Gallaudet College.
1947—Rhulin Thomas flies solo across the U.S.A.
1950—First transistor hearing aid available for deaf people.
1954—California School for the Deaf at Riverside opens (California's second residential school).
  —U.S. Supreme Court ends racial segregation in all schools.
  —The Columbia Institution is renamed Gallaudet College.
1955—Crotched Mountain School for the Deaf opens in New Hampshire.
1956—NAD reorganizes to improve.
  —National Congress of Jewish Deaf is organized.
1957—Wyoming School for the Deaf opens in Casper.
1958—President Dwight D. Eisenhower establishes Captioned Films for the Deaf by signing Public Law 85-905.
1959—Gallaudet College publishes book *Occupational Conditions Among the Deaf.*

Chapter 6

The 1960s
(*Deaf Heritage*, pp. 317–356)

Jr. National Association
of the Deaf

At the 1960 Convention of the National Association of the Deaf, the idea of the Junior National Association of the Deaf, (Jr. NAD) was born. Mrs. Caroline Burnes, wife of NAD President Byron B. Burnes, *proposed* the idea. She suggested that the NAD organize a Jr. NAD chapter in schools for the deaf. The purpose of the youth organization was simple: to develop new leaders among the young deaf people in the schools.

Mervin D. Garretson, principal of the Montana School for the Deaf, was *appointed* director of the new project. He worked with a committee. The members of the committee were Lawrence Newman (California School for the Deaf at Riverside), Marvin S. Rood (West Virginia School for the Deaf), G. Dewey Coats (Missouri School for the Deaf), and Caroline Burnes (California School for the Deaf at Berkeley).

During the first year, Jr. NAD chapters were established at six schools for the deaf.

These chapters were at the schools where the committee members and Committee Chairman Garretson worked.

In 1962, Mervin Garretson moved to Washington, D.C., to join the faculty of Gallaudet College. Mrs. Viola McDowell of Montana *succeeded* Garretson as Jr. NAD Director. In 1965, she was succeeded by Richard Tuma of New Jersey. In 1966, the Jr. NAD national headquarters moved to Gallaudet College, and Frank R. Turk was chosen National Director. Turk held the position for 12 years. In 1980, Melinda Padden, a teacher at the Maryland School for the Deaf, succeeded Turk.

Over the years, the Jr. NAD grew quickly. By the 1970s it had over 3,000 members and nearly 100 chapters. In 1962, publication of a Jr. NAD magazine began. It was first called *The Jr. NAD* and was later renamed *The Junior Deaf American*.

The goals of the Junior NAD are to develop young deaf leaders and to encourage deaf

Caroline Burnes

youth to excel. The organization established several awards to encourage deaf students. The awards are named for deaf adult leaders. Some of the awards are: Lawrence Newman Award for Journalism; Loy Golladay Award for Essay Writing; Robert Panara Award for Poetry; Byron B. Burnes Award for Leadership. There are many other awards, too.

> ## Vocabulary
> proposed—V—suggested
> appointed—V—picked; selected
> succeeded—V—replaced

More About the Jr. NAD

In May, 1968, the Jr. National Association of the Deaf held its first national convention. The convention was at Gallaudet College, and 120 deaf students and their advisors attended. Since then, national conventions have been held in 1970 at Gallaudet College, in 1972 at the National Technical Institute for the Deaf (NTID), in 1974 at Gallaudet College, in 1976 at the North Carolina School for the Deaf, in 1978 at Swan Lake Lodge in Pengilly, Minnesota, in 1980 at the NAD Centennial Convention in Cincinnati, Ohio, and in 1982 at NTID.

Since 1968, there have been other conferences as well. In 1968, the first national Youth Leadership Conference was held at the Indiana School for the Deaf. It was led by Gary Olsen. The second Youth Leadership Conference was in 1969 at the Texas School for the Deaf in Austin. After that, conferences were held every two years. They were regional, not national. There was an Eastern Deaf Youth Conference and a Western Deaf Youth Conference. These conferences have been held at many different schools for the deaf: Governor Baxter School in Maine; Washington State School; and at schools in the following states: Maryland, Minnesota, South Carolina, Oregon, California (Berkeley), Indiana, New Jersey, Montana, and Massachusetts.

In 1969, the Jr. NAD held its first four-week Youth Leadership Development Camp in Pennsylvania. The following year, the camp was held at Swan Lake Lodge in Pengilly, Minnesota. It has continued *annually* at the Minnesota location since 1970. Hundreds of deaf youth are alumni of the camp, now run by Roger Claussen.

Jr. NAD chapters have been involved in their local *communities* by raising funds, planning deaf *awareness* programs, and collecting food and clothing for poor families. Their programs have helped hearing people in the community to understand deaf people better.

Many *former* Jr. NAD members have become successful deaf adults. Melinda Chapel Padden was the chairperson of the first Youth Leadership Conference. She later became the director of the Jr. NAD! Many other deaf leaders today got their start with the Jr. NAD chapter at their school.

The Telephone Arrives

In 1964, Robert Weitbrecht invented the acoustic coupler. Using old teletypewriters with the acoustic couplers made telephones accessible to deaf people. Weitbrecht was a deaf electronic scientist in California. He died in June, 1983.

Although Alexander Graham Bell invented the telephone in 1876, deaf people could not benefit from his invention. It took almost 90 years before deaf people could use telephones. When Bell invented the phone, he had hoped it would help deaf people. Instead, it became a *barrier*. Many deaf people have been told they could not be promoted in their work because they could not use the telephone. Some were told they had to be able to use the phone to get a new job. Deaf people have also had to ask hearing people to make telephone calls for them. For many deaf people the telephone has been a *hindrance* and has meant a loss of privacy.

Teletypewriters are machines with a typewriter keyboard. When one key is tapped, the same key on another keyboard is *activated*. This is how a message is sent and received. These machines have been used to send news, weather reports, and telegrams, and they are now making telephones accessible to deaf people. Now many new machines have been developed for use by deaf people with the telephone; they are called *TDDs* — telecommunication devices for the deaf.

Since 1964, services for TDD users have grown. Deaf people can now call a special number at many companies to get information or to order something. They can call the telephone company for help with a telephone number; they can call train stations or airlines. Hospitals and police departments in many cities have TDDs, and agencies that work with deaf people often have answering services for deaf people. The deaf person can call on a TDD, and the answering service will call a hearing person using voice. In this way, deaf people can call hearing friends who do not have TDDs.

The first teletypewriters (TTYs) were very large, but many changes have been made in the machines since the 1960s. Deaf people can now buy very small and *compact models* that run on batteries. There are many different companies and models to choose from.

Registry of Interpreters for the Deaf

During the summer of 1964, a workshop was held in Muncie, Indiana. The Workshop on Interpreting for the Deaf was chaired by Dr. Edgar L. Lowell. He was the *administrator* of the John Tracy Clinic. The *participants* decided to establish an organization of interpreters. Originally, the name chosen was National Registry of Professional Interpreters and Translators for the Deaf. Later, the name was shortened to Registry of Interpreters for the Deaf, RID.

RID, the *commonly* used name for the new organization, grew quickly. In the past, interpreters were not paid. They were often friends or family members of the deaf person. After RID was established, interpreting became a profession. The Registry continued to develop the field of interpreting by having *evaluations*. The evaluations tested an interpreter's skills. If interpreters passed the evaluation, they received RID *Certification*. This method of evaluating the skills of an interpreter is still being used today.

The RID opened a national headquarters in Silver Spring, Maryland. The organization offers workshops that help interpreters improve their signing skills and workshops for deaf people, too, so they know how to use interpreters. The National RID publishes a newspaper that is sent to every member. The RID has made interpreting a field of *professionals*, not *volunteers*.

Many states in the U.S. have registries of interpreters or *commissions* where interpreters can be obtained. Deaf people attending colleges, needing to see their lawyers or doctors, appearing in court, or watching theatre can obtain interpreters today. Plays on Broadway in New York are now regularly performed with interpreted shows. Political speeches have been made with an interpreter signing the speech for deaf people. Religious and news programs on television often have interpreters, too.

Interpreting Certificates can be earned for different skills. A Comprehensive Skills Certificate (CSC) is awarded to an interpreter who demonstrates both expressive and receptive signing skills. In addition, CSC interpreters must follow a Code of Ethics. This is a set of rules for interpreters. For example, certified interpreters must not tell anyone what happens or is discussed between a deaf client and a hearing client. This is called *confidentiality*. They must always interpret only what is said by the deaf person and the hearing person. An interpreter cannot add his or her own opinion. There are other rules in the Code of Ethics that a certified interpreter must obey.

Deaf people can become certified by RID, too. A Reverse Skills Certificate (RSC) is awarded to a qualified deaf person who has skills in both signed English and American Sign Language.

There are other types of certificates that interpreters can earn. These include interpreting for oral deaf people, theatrical productions, and legal situations.

Vocabulary

administrator—N—director; leader

participants—N—people who join an activity; people present at a workshop

commonly—ADV—often used

evaluations—N—examinations; tests

certification—N—proof of passing an exam or evaluation

professionals—N—people who are paid for doing a job

volunteers—N—people who do a job without being paid

commission—N—office or agency

confidentiality—N—keeping secret; not discussing something that is private

Cued Speech

During the *decade* of the sixties, a new term entered the *vocabulary* of deaf education. It described a new system of teaching speech to deaf children. "Cued Speech" was developed by Dr. Orin Cornett of Gallaudet College.

Cued Speech refers to special visual clues used to help a deaf person speechread. Eight different handshapes (*cues*) are positioned in four different places around the lips, on the face and neck. The cues represent sounds of spoken language.

Cues make it possible for hearing parents to communicate more *visually*. Cued Speech is not sign language, and it does not use any signs. It is a system of showing sounds that cannot be seen on the lips.

Vocabulary

decade—N—10-year period of time
vocabulary—N—collection of words
cues—N—handshapes (they are not
   signs) that help a person speechread
visually—ADV—describing something
   that is easily seen

The Council of Organizations Serving the Deaf

The Council of Organizations Serving the Deaf, *COSD*, was founded in New York City in 1967. COSD was established to give different *agencies* and organizations a chance to meet and talk about deafness. Many different organizations were working to improve services for the deaf at that time. Unfortunately, they were not working together.

The U.S. Department of Health, Education, and Welfare gave COSD a five-year grant. Mervin Garretson, a faculty member of Gallaudet College, was hired as the first executive director of COSD.

The Council of Organizations Serving the Deaf grew and at one time had members from 18 national organizations. Several national *forums* were held that had *themes* related to deafness. In 1970, Executive Director Garretson left his position with COSD to become principal of the Model Secondary School for the Deaf in Washington, D.C. Edward Carney became the second executive director.

Mervin Garretson

Executive Director Carney applied for a three-year *extension* of the grant. He was given the grant, but eight months later the government decided to end its support of COSD. At the same time, many other programs for deaf people were losing support. The Council had to close its office, and soon after that the organization *folded*.

Vocabulary

agencies—N—offices or organizations in
   the field of human service, social
   work, etc.
forum—N—workshop or conference
themes—N—purposes for meeting
extension—N—continuation; more time
folded—V—closed permanently

Deaf Administrators

Until the 1960s there were very few deaf people in *administrative* positions. As that decade progressed, more and more deaf people moved into these positions. The National Association of the Deaf moved its offices to Washington, D.C.

and Frederick Schreiber was named executive secretary. Schreiber was deaf. Many other people rose to supervisory positions. Albert Pimentel became the director of the Registry of Interpreters for the Deaf and Mervin Garretson the executive director of the Council of Organizations Serving the Deaf. Terrence J. O'Rourke became head of the NAD Communicative Skills Program. Jack R. Gannon was hired as the first executive secretary of the Gallaudet College Alumni Association.

These administrators proved that deaf people could hold positions of leadership and responsibility. In the years after these people were hired, many other deaf people became administrators in education, *rehabilitation*, social work, and other fields.

National Theatre for the Deaf

Bernard Bragg

The National Theatre of the Deaf

In 1967, a new *era* in American theatre arrived. The National Theatre of the Deaf was established that year because of many people's hard work.

The idea of a theatre for deaf actors had been suggested since the 1950s. At that time, a hearing actress, Anne Bancroft, had to learn sign language for a part she was playing. Ms. Bancroft played the role of Annie Sullivan in *The Miracle Worker*. While involved in that project, Ms. Bancroft met Dr. Edna Levine. Dr. Levine was a psychologist who worked with deaf people.

Dr. Levine, Anne Bancroft, and a man named Arthur Penn wrote a *proposal*. The proposal was *submitted* to the federal government. The three hoped to obtain money to establish a theatre of the deaf. Their proposal was turned down.

Later, a man named David Hays contacted Dr. Levine about a special project he was doing. He had the idea of a theatre using *visual language*. Levine introduced Hays to Bernard Bragg, a deaf actor who had studied *mime* in France. Bragg travelled to many places to perform and had a television show each week called *The Quiet Man*.

When Hays and Bragg met, they decided to work together on a proposal. They submitted the proposal to the U.S. Department of Health, Education, and Welfare. The grant was approved and gave the two men the money to establish the National Theatre of the Deaf.

Since that time, the National Theatre of the Deaf has appeared all over the world. Thousands of people have seen the *troupe* perform. There have been television specials and international tours. Several of the actors and actresses have been in movies and television shows. Linda Bove is on *Sesame Street* regularly and was also on the soap opera, *Search*

Phyllis A. Frelich

for Tomorrow. Bernard Bragg, Audree Norton, Tim Scanlon, Ed Waterstreet, and Phyllis Frelich have all become well-known deaf performers in television or theatrical *productions.* Phyllis Frelich went on to win a *Tony Award* on Broadway for her role in the drama, *Children of a Lesser God.*

Today, sign language does not carry a *stigma.* It is respected as a language and is used in most schools for the deaf. On stage and on television, sign language is beautiful, artful, and expressive. Thousands of Americans have started to learn how to sign. The popularity of sign language has helped deaf people feel proud to be deaf and proud of their language.

Bernard Bragg once said "People used to push my hands down in embarrassment and tell me not to sign. Now people pay to see me perform in sign language!"

Vocabulary

era—N—period of time
proposal—N—a request for money to do a special project
submitted—V—given
visual language—N—communicating without sound; a language that can only be seen
mime—N—pantomime; acting without language
troupe—N—theatre company
productions—N—shows
Tony Award—N—a special honorary award for outstanding work in theatre
stigma—N—bad or negative image

Time-Line
1960–1969

1960—Riverside City College in California begins program for the deaf.
—National Association of the Deaf forms Jr. NAD.
—Federal government provides stipends for teacher training.
—Northern Illinois University at DeKalb establishes program for hearing- and speech-impaired people.

1961—Leadership Training Program in the area of the deaf begins at San Fernando Valley State College.

1964—Registry of Interpreters for the Deaf is established.
—Alexander Graham Bell Association forms Oral Deaf Adults section.
—Robert Weitbrecht invents the acoustic coupler.
—California State University at Northridge opens program for deaf students.
—State Technical Institute and Rehabilitation Center Plainwell, Michigan, opens deaf services.

1965—American Athletic Association of the Deaf holds 10th International Games for the Deaf in Washington, D.C.
—Eastern North Carolina School for the Deaf opens in Wilson.

1966—Professional Rehabilitation Workers with the Adult Deaf organized.
—St. Petersburg Junior College in Clearwater, Florida, opens program for deaf students.
—National Theatre of the Deaf opens.
—New York University opens Deafness Research and Training Center.

1967—Council of Organizations Serving the Deaf established in New York City.
—Communicative Skills Program begins under the NAD.
—National Theatre of the Deaf goes on first national tour.

1968—Community College of Denver offers program for the hearing impaired.
—Alexander Graham Bell Association and National Association of the Deaf work together to establish Teletypewriters for the Deaf, Inc. in Indiana.
—National Technical Institute for the Deaf opens at Rochester Institute of Technology.
—Delgado Junior College in New Orleans opens programs for the deaf.
—National Theatre of the Deaf adds Little Theatre of the Deaf.
—U.S. Congress authorizes funding for the Model Secondary School for the Deaf at Gallaudet College.
—Utah State University, Logan, Utah, offers program for hearing-impaired students.
—Permanent Alumni Office opens at Gallaudet College.

1969—Seattle Community College begins programs for the deaf.
—Dr. Edward C. Merrill, Jr. becomes fourth president of Gallaudet College.
—Lee College, Baytown, Texas, offers programs for the deaf.
—National Theatre of the Deaf goes on first European tour.
—Tennessee Temple School for the Deaf opens in Chattanooga.
—St. Paul Technical Vocational Institute opens in St. Paul, Minnesota.

Chapter 7

Our Deaf World

(Deaf Heritage, pp. 203–210; 251; 269; 380)

Deaf people, like hearing people, tell stories and jokes. Sometimes the stories are funny, and sometimes they are sad. Both happy and sad stories are about life and what happens to people. Deaf people's stories are often about life as a deaf person. In this section, you will read some stories, poems, jokes, and anecdotes that were written by deaf people. The funny ones poke fun at being deaf. The sad ones show the misunderstandings and the hard parts of being deaf.

Hazards of Deafness

In the early 1970s, Roy Holcomb started to write a list. He was working at the Program for the Deaf in Santa Ana, California, as the area supervisor. Holcomb's list was made of experiences common to deaf people. His anecdotes, or short stories about being deaf, have been published in book form—*Hazards of Deafness.* The first publication was called *95 Hazards of Deafness,* but it has been expanded, and the book is now in its third edition. (See *Deaf Heritage—Hazards,* pp. 209–210.)

9. A pebble gets into your hub cap and you go 800 miles before someone brings it to your attention.

41. You are waiting for an elevator and one opens in back of or to the side of you and you fail to notice it. Do you feel funny when you do see it! Then it is just your luck to have the door close on you as you get halfway to the elevator.

60. You pay full admission to movies, night clubs, or other places where sound of one kind or another is an important part of the price. Then you sit back and "watch" what your money has bought.

64. You watch a football game for ages wondering what the score is before it is finally flashed on the screen.

69. At the movies you laugh aloud when others cry and cry when others laugh, because you don't see things the same as other people hear them in the movies.

83. You are in a crowd of a thousand people and feel more alone than if you were standing in the middle of the Sahara Desert.

97. You put dishes and silverware away as if there was an earthquake, never realizing that you are making so much noise.

105. You are trapped all alone in an elevator and can't talk with anyone on the emergency phone or on the outside. You just hope people are trying to get to you even if you can't hear them.

128. Your hearing aid leaks and makes a beeping noise. People look at you as if you were a doctor and your beeper is going off and you should call in to your office immediately.

138. You type away and don't hear the bell at the end of the carriage and many of your words end up beyond your right margin stop.

174. You are a star football quarterback. You take the ball through the middle, throwing opponents right and left as you go seventy yards for a touchdown, only to find that the whistle was blown twenty yards back where a clipping penalty occurred.

296. You are eight years old and playing a game of hide and seek. When you finally get brave enough to return to the base, you find that the game was over a half hour ago, and everyone went home.

Proppaganda

George Propp graduated from the Nebraska School for the Deaf and later returned to that school to teach. He earned a doctoral degree from the University of Nebraska and served as president of the Convention of American Instructors of the Deaf. His extracurricular activities have included the column "Proppaganda" in *The Nebraska Journal*. (See *Deaf Heritage*, p. 251.)

Proppaganda by George Propp
The best friend of the deaf is not the fellow who gives them advice and assistance. It is the man who asks them for it.

* * *

Fractured Bromides—*Every silver lining has a dark cloud: We read somewhere not long ago that Navy research has shown that subjects with a certain type of nerve deafness can't get seasick. They can't, on a dark night, pass a standard sobriety test either.*

* * *

A recent publication warns us that the telephone is about to become a reality for deaf people. By George, there goes another of our advantages.

* * *

They're having a workshop for interpreters in the near future. Shouldn't they have one for the speakers first? Then, in logical sequence, have one for interpreters and finally another for people like us who can't stay awake during speeches?

* * *

A $14,000 research project at the University of Pittsburgh reveals that children who learn the sign language early have better educational achievement. By George, Ed Scouten told us nearly the same thing about fifteen years ago and he didn't charge us a dime.

* * *

On the other hand, our hearing friends also possess some advantages. At least we've never heard of a hearing worker who had to stick his "vocal organs" into the maw of a 75-ton press.

* * *

An eighth-grade boy with an ear ache was sent to the infirmary. He came back cured and told his teacher, "Boy, I was really worried. I thought I was becoming deaf!"

You Have To Be Deaf To Understand

"You Have To Be Deaf To Understand" was written by Willard Madsen in 1971. The author graduated from the Kansas School for the Deaf and is an associate professor at Gallaudet College. The poem has been read and loved by thousands of people. It has also been translated into seven foreign languages. (See *Deaf Heritage*, p. 380.)

You Have to be Deaf to Understand
By Willard J. Madsen

What is it like to "hear" a hand?
You have to be deaf to understand.

What is it like to be a small child,
In a school, in a room void of sound—
With a teacher who talks and talks and talks;
And then when she does come around to you,
She expects you to know what she's said?
You have to be deaf to understand.

Or the teacher thinks that to make you smart,
You must first learn how to talk with your voice;
So mumbo-jumbo with hands on your face
For hours and hours without patience or end,
Until out comes a faint resembling sound?
You have to be deaf to understand.

What is it like to be curious,
To thirst for knowledge you can call your own,
With an inner desire that's set on fire—
And you ask a brother, sister, or friend
Who looks in answer and says, "Never mind"?
You have to be deaf to understand.

What is it like in a corner to stand,
Though there's nothing you've done really wrong,
Other than try to make use of your hands
To a silent peer to communicate
A thought that comes to your mind all at once?
You have to be deaf to understand.

What is it like to be shouted at
When one thinks that will help you to hear;
Or misunderstand the words of a friend
Who is trying to make a joke clear,
And you don't get the point because he's failed?
You have to be deaf to understand.

What is it like to be laughed in the face
When you try to repeat what is said;
Just to make sure that you've understood,
And you find that the words were misread—
And you want to cry out, "Please help me, friend"?
You have to be deaf to understand.

What is it like to have to depend
Upon one who can hear to phone a friend;
Or place a call to a business firm
And be forced to share what's personal, and,
Then find that your message wasn't made clear?
You have to be deaf to understand.

What is it like to be deaf and alone
In the company of those who can hear—
And you only guess as you go along,
For no one's there with a helping hand,
As you try to keep up with words and song?
You have to be deaf to understand.

What is it like on the road of life
To meet with a stranger who opens his mouth—
And speaks out a line at a rapid pace;
And you can't understand the look in his face
Because it is new and you're lost in the race?
You have to be deaf to understand.

What is it like to comprehend
Some nimble fingers that paint the scene,
And make you smile and feel serene
With the "spoken word" of the moving hand
That makes you part of the world at large?
You have to be deaf to understand.

What is it like to "hear" a hand?
Yes, you have to be deaf to understand.

Willard J. Madsen

On His Deafness

Robert Panara was the first deaf professional hired by the National Technical Institute for the Deaf in 1967. He helped establish the NTID English department and organized the NTID Drama Club, now called the Experimental Educational Theatre. (See *Deaf Heritage*, p. 269.)

On His Deafness
by Robert F. Panara

My ears are deaf, and yet I seem to hear
Sweet nature's music and the songs of man,
For I have learned from Fancy's artisan
How written words can thrill the inner ear
Just as they move the heart, and so for me
They also seem to ring out loud and free.
In silent study, I have learned to tell
Each secret shade of meaning, and to hear
A magic harmony, at once sincere,
That somehow notes the tinkle of a bell,
The cooing of a dove, the swish of leaves,
The raindrop's pitter-patter on the eaves,
The lover's sigh, and thrumming of guitar—
And if I choose, the rustle of a star!

Robert Panara

Chapter 8

Publications

(*Deaf Heritage*, pp. 237–254)

Educational Publications of the Deaf

The first educational publication was established in 1847. Members of the faculty at the American Asylum for the Deaf proposed starting a *periodical* that would be printed four times per year. The purpose of the periodical was to discuss topics related to deafness. The school approved the idea and the periodical was started. It was called *The American Annals of the Deaf*. It is still being printed today and is the oldest educational *journal* in the country. It is also the oldest periodical about deafness in the world!

From 1847 to 1875, 10 educational publications of the deaf were established. In 1849, the North Carolina School for the Deaf started *The Deaf Mute*. Today, it is called *The North Carolinian*.

At the Ohio School for the Deaf, *The Mute* was first printed in 1868. It is known today as *The Ohio Chronicle*. Illinois School for the Deaf began *The Deaf Mute Advance*, now called *The Illinois Advance*, in 1870. *The Kentucky Deaf-Mute*, published by the Kentucky School for the Deaf, was published in 1874. It is *The Kentucky Standard* now.

Three other periodicals began in 1874: *The Deaf-Mute Mirror*, now *The Michigan Mirror*; *The Mute Journal of Nebraska Deaf*, now *The Nebraska Journal*; and *The Goodson Gazette*, now *The Virginia Guide*. The next year, *The Colorado Index* and *The Kansas Star* were founded.

Vocabulary

periodical—N—a newspaper or magazine printed at established periods of time

journal—N—a periodical; newspaper or magazine

Periodicals for and by Deaf People

In 1860, the first periodical for deaf people began. It was *The Gallaudet Guide and Deaf Mutes' Companion*. It was printed each

VOLUME LVIII Published Every Thursday, at 99 Ft. Washington Ave. **NEW YORK, THURSDAY, DECEMBER 5, 1929** Subscription Price, $1 a year. **NUMBER 49**

Entered as second class matter January 6, 1922, at the Post Office at New York, N.Y., under the Act of March 3, 1879. "There are more men ennobled by reading than by nature." Acceptance for mailing at special rate of postage provided for in Section 1103, Act of October 3, 1917, authorized on July 18, 1918.

Mast head of the old Deaf-Mutes' Journal

month and edited by William Chamberlain. It was printed in Boston from 1860–1865. The *banner* of the *Guide* showed pictures of Thomas Hopkins Gallaudet and Laurent Clerc. It was the official newspaper of the New England Gallaudet Association of the Deaf.

In 1875, the independent printing of *The Deaf-Mutes' Journal* started. The publisher was Henry C. Rider. This newspaper became the first weekly newspaper for the deaf community. Later, the publishing was taken over by the New York School for the Deaf. Edwin Hodgson, the school's printing teacher, became editor. He was editor of *The Deaf-Mutes' Journal* for 53 years, 1878–1931. Under Hodgson, *The Deaf-Mutes' Journal* became very popular. After Hodgson left his job as editor, Thomas F. Fox succeeded him. The name of the newspaper was changed to *New York Journal of the Deaf.* Publication of this newspaper stopped in 1951.

In 1871, four men worked together to establish a literary magazine for deaf people. Melville Ballard, John B. Hotchkiss, Joseph B. Parkinson, and James Denison teamed up to start *The Silent World.* It was published in Washington, D.C., but it was only printed for five years. Many people said that it ended because deaf people did not *appreciate* its "literary nature."

The National Exponent was first published in 1894. Some excellent deaf writers were on the staff of this newspaper: Robert McGregor, James Cloud, and J. Shuyler Long as well as George W. Veditz and James Gallagher. O.H.

Regensburg owned the company. *The National Exponent* had over 1,200 readers when it was most successful, but it went out of business in 1896.

George S. Porter was a very well-known publisher. He was a student at the New York School for the Deaf as a child and started to learn printing there. One of his teachers was Edwin Hodgson, editor of *The Deaf Mutes' Journal.* When Porter graduated from the New York School for the Deaf in 1884, he went into the printing field. He lived in New York and then moved to Arkansas. Porter taught printing at the Arkansas School for the Deaf. From Arkansas, he moved to Trenton, New Jersey, to teach printing and work on the local newspaper. At that time, the newspaper was very small and was called *The Deaf-Mute Times.* After a few issues, Porter changed the name of the newspaper to *The Silent Worker.* Gradually, the newspaper improved. Instead of being only four pages, it grew to be the best magazine deaf readers had ever seen!

The Silent Worker was filled with interesting stories about deaf and hearing leaders, histories of schools for the deaf, travel information, and news. There were photographs by deaf photographers and pictures by deaf artists.

Porter decided to retire in 1928 after 36 years, and one year later the magazine ended. In 1948, it began again under the NAD and is now called *The Deaf American.*

Other publications that were written by and for deaf people came and went. *The*

American Deaf Citizen started in 1929 and stopped being published in 1942. *The Modern Silents* began in Texas in 1937 and ended in 1939. *The Digest of the Deaf* began in Massachusetts in 1938 and was in publication until 1940. *The Silent Cavalier* began in Virginia in 1943 but later *merged* with other periodicals.

The Silent News, a monthly newspaper, began appearing in 1969. It is still being printed and has over 3,000 readers.

The Buff and Blue

In 1892, a group of students at Gallaudet College started a monthly magazine. They named their periodical *The Buff and Blue.* The magazine was written, edited, and printed by the college students. It later changed from a magazine to a newspaper *format.*

Many well-known deaf adults were once on the staff of *The Buff and Blue.* While at college, these people became interested in *journalism.* When they left Gallaudet, their interest in writing, printing, or publishing continued. Former *editors* of *The Buff and Blue* went on to become editors of other newspapers. Some of them were: Byron B. Burnes (*The Companion* and *California News*); Loy Golladay (*The West Virginia Tablet* and *The American Era*); and Jack R. Gannon (*The Nebraska Journal*).

Other students who had been active on *The Buff and Blue* became involved in other literary work. James Sowell published a collection of his poetry. Thomas Ulmer also wrote poetry and an *autobiography.* Terrence J.

O'Rourke wrote several books on sign language and opened his own publishing company called T.J. Publishers. Robert F. Panara, John H. McFarlane, and Taras Denis worked together to write *Silent Muse: An Anthology of Poetry and Prose by the Deaf,* which was published by the Gallaudet College Alumni Association in 1960.

Rex Lowman, Mervin Garretson, Willard Madsen, Linwood Smith, and Dorothy Miles were all editors of *The Buff and Blue* as well. All have written poetry which has been published. Madsen's poem, "You Have To Be Deaf To Understand" can be found in this book.

The Buff and Blue has strongly influenced deafness-related journalism since 1892. Leading deaf writers got their start with the Gallaudet College publication. The newspaper is still in existence and is almost 100 years old!

Literary Efforts of Deaf Persons

James Nack became deaf at the age of eight after he fell down a flight of stairs. He later became the first deaf man to publish a book in America. His book was an *anthology* of poems that he wrote. The 68 poems were written while Nack was only 14 to 17 years old! The collection of poetry was published in 1827 and was titled *Legend of the*

Rock and Other Pieces. During Nack's life, he wrote three more books of poetry.

Since Nack's book was published, many other deaf authors have emerged. In 1974, *The Gallaudet Almanac* listed over 100 books written by deaf people! The books have been about history, science fiction, and sports; they have included autobiographies and *biographies, novels,* sign language texts, and poetry.

Vocabulary

anthology—N—collection
biography—N—a story or book about a
    person's life written by someone else
novel—N—a book that is made-up, not
    true; a fictional book

Published Deaf Authors

Howard L. Terry, who died in 1964, was a very *prolific* deaf author. He wrote his first story when he was only 12 years old and sewed the pages together to make a book. Two years later, he completed the story which was later published. By the time he was 21, Terry had written three books. He also wrote poetry, stories, and drama and had many of these published. He attended Gallaudet College and was awarded an *honorary degree* in 1938 for his contributions to the field of literature.

Some other deaf people and their works in literature are listed below. There are many others, not included here, who have also had their work published. *Verses* by Mary Peet (1903); *A Deaf Mute Howls* by Albert Ballin (1930); *The Law and the Deaf* by Lowell Myers (1967); *Deafness* by Alan Crammatte (1968); *Deaf Heritage* by Jack R. Gannon (1981); *A Deaf Adult Speaks Out* by Leo Jacobs (1977).

Vocabulary

prolific—ADJ—productive; inventive
honorary degree—N—a degree given by
    a college to someone who did not
    study for the degree but who has been
    very successful in life

Chapter 9

American Sign Language: Our Natural Language

(Deaf Heritage, pp. 357–376)

"The Noblest Gift"

George W. Veditz was the seventh president of the National Association of the Deaf. He was proud of his language, American Sign Language. He is quoted for what he once said when he talked about signing. He said that "sign language was God's *noblest* gift to deaf people."

We do not know exactly when people first started to sign. History has traced sign language back over 1,000 years. We know that in Italy, in the year 530 A.D., *monks* used signs to communicate. They made *vows* of silence as part of their religion. They were not allowed to speak. Instead of using their voices, they made up signs to *communicate*.

Two famous monks were also teachers of the deaf. Pedro Ponce de Leon, in Spain, taught deaf students using signs. Abbe de l'Epee, in France, also taught deaf children using signs. He established a new system of sign language using signs that he learned from deaf people and French grammar.

Thomas H. Gallaudet met a teacher at the school de l'Epee established in France. That teacher was Laurent Clerc. The two men brought French signs with them when they travelled to America in 1816. Their school for deaf children in Connecticut used both French signs and the local American signs already being used. The mixed language later spread to other schools for the deaf and is today what we call American Sign Language!

Vocabulary

noblest—ADJ—greatest; grandest; highest

monks—N—religious men who live a very strict life serving God

vows—N—promises

communicate—V—express thoughts and ideas

Dr. Stokoe at work in his lab at Gallaudet College.

American Sign Language Comes Out of the Closet

Dr. William C. Stokoe, Jr., was hired by Gallaudet College in the mid-1950s. He became the chairman of the English Department. After he was at Gallaudet and saw the way deaf people communicated, Dr. Stokoe became interested in sign language. Sign language was the way most students at Gallaudet communicated, and Dr. Stokoe was fascinated. He was a hearing person, and signs were new to him.

Dr. Stokoe decided to propose a study of sign language. Many other teachers were not interested, though, and thought Dr. Stokoe was crazy to think about studying sign language. Even deaf teachers were not very interested in the project. Dr. Stokoe did not give up when other people were *indifferent*. Instead, he started the *Linguistics* Research Program in 1957. Stokoe and two assistants worked on this project during the summer and after school.

Carl Croneberg and Dorothy Casterline who are both deaf, were Dr. Stokoe's assistants for the Linguistics Research Program. The three *researchers* made films of deaf people signing. The deaf people in the films did not understand what the research was about and were just trying to be nice to Dr. Stokoe. Many people thought the whole project was silly, but *humored* Dr. Stokoe anyway.

Stokoe and his team studied the films of signing. They *analyzed* the films and tried to see patterns in the signs. The results of the research were a big surprise. They found that the signs followed *specific* rules. They found that the rules were used by all of the signers and were linguistic rules.

Dr. Stokoe was the first linguist to test Sign Language as a real language. It passed all of the tests! Dr. Stokoe published the results in 1960, but not many people paid attention to the study. Dr. Stokoe was still alone—he was the only linguist who believed sign language was more than *gestures*. He knew it was a language *in its own right* and not another form of English.

Vocabulary

indifferent—ADJ—apathetic; not interested

linguistics—N—the study of languages

researchers—N—people who are involved in an experiment

humored—V—agreeing with a person when you don't really agree; nodding when you don't really agree

analyzed—V—studied every little part carefully

specific—ADJ—exact

gestures—N—moving the hands to describe something without using real signs; mime

"in its own right"—by itself

The Continuing Work of Dr. William C. Stokoe, Jr.

In 1965, Dr. Stokoe and his two assistants published a book. The book was called *A Dictionary of American Sign Language on Linguistic Principles*. After the book was published, many people became interested in studying signs and the language itself. Dr. Stokoe's work made sign language a *legitimate* and acceptable *topic* for research. Other hearing linguists became involved in the study of American Sign Language. A few deaf people also became interested in linguistics because of Dr. Stokoe's research. These deaf people later published their own books about linguistics and American Sign Language.

In 1973, James Woodward completed his *dissertation* at Georgetown University. His dissertation was on American Sign Language, and he became the first linguist to earn a *doctorate* in that subject.

The researchers who have studied American Sign Language report that it has its own rules of grammar. It can be used to describe anything that any other language describes. Some people said that sign language could not be used for *abstract* concepts like "hate", "pity", "death", etc., but research proved that American Sign Language can express abstract thought.

Researchers proved something else: if the signs are written in English and look wrong, it is *not* because American Sign Language is *sloppy* or poor English. Many other languages look the same way if they are translated word for word into English. For example, German, Chinese, and Russian have different grammar from English.

In 1980, Dr. Stokoe's friends and *colleagues* got together. They planned a surprise to honor his work. They wrote special articles to be put together in a book. The book, *Sign Language and the Deaf Community: Essays in Honor of William C. Stokoe*, was presented to Dr. Stokoe in 1980 at the NAD Convention. The money earned from selling this book is put into the William C. Stokoe Scholarship Fund. The scholarship encourages continued research into American Sign Language.

Vocabulary

legitimate—ADJ—real, genuine, honorable and good

topic—N—idea for research or discussion

dissertation—N—research paper required before a person earns a Ph.D.; thesis paper

doctorate—N—the highest university degree one can earn; Ph.D., Ed.D.

abstract—ADJ—a thought; something you cannot touch that is real

sloppy—ADJ—confused, unorganized, messy

colleagues—N—other people in the same profession; co-workers

The Growth of Interest

Since William Stokoe, Jr. proved that American Sign Language is a *true language*, many changes have taken place. The changes have been in *attitudes*. Many people used to think that deaf people had no *culture*. People often believed that the language of deaf people was "broken English" or "bad English." Now we know that American Sign Language is not English at all!

Carol Padden is a hearing impaired *linguist*. She once said that researchers had never studied the culture of deaf people because many people thought deaf people did not have a culture! Now much more is known about the "Deaf Community," and new research is being done everyday. *Sign Language and the Deaf Community*, the book honoring Stokoe, is a good example of this research. There are many articles in the book which connect American Sign Language to Deaf Culture.

Deaf people have had the opportunity to get involved in teaching classes to sign students. The National Association of the Deaf created a series of classes in American Sign Language in 1967. The classes were named the Communicative Skills Program and directed by a deaf teacher. The director's name was Terrence J. O'Rourke. In 1975, this organization established SIGN—Sign Instructor's Guidance Network. This group of professional sign language teachers was given the *authority* to certify teachers. The teachers of American Sign Language had to be evaluated by the SIGN to receive their certification. This helped to *guarantee* the *quality* of classes.

In 1978, O'Rourke left his position with the Communicative Skills Program. He decided to open his own publishing business. Another deaf man, S. Melvin Carter, Jr. took over. That year, the Communicative Skills Program added a new program. The new addition was a training program for teachers. Ella Mae Lentz was hired as coordinator of the new program.

Edna Adler, a deaf consultant with the federal government, believes that this program of the Communicative Skills Program was important. It helped people think positively about American Sign Language . . ."more than anything else it helped remove the stigma of using sign language . . ."

Vocabulary

"true language"—N—a separate language with its own rules and vocabulary

attitudes—N—feelings about something; the way people think

culture—N—the special behaviors, attitudes, and language of a group of people

linguist—N—a person who studies languages

network—N—system; contacts

authority—N—power; permission

guarantee—V—promise

quality—N—value; how good something is

Chapter 10

The 1970's
(*Deaf Heritage*, pp. 377–417)

The Miss Deaf America Pageant

During the 1970s, a beauty *pageant* for deaf women started. It was the Miss Deaf America Pageant; beautiful deaf women from various states *competed*. The first contest was in 1972 at the National Association of the Deaf Convention in Miami, Florida. The winner of the first competition was Ann Billington. She represented Gallaudet College at the pageant.

The contest has been held every two years since 1972. The 1974 pageant was at the NAD Convention in Seattle, Washington, and the winner was Mary Pearce, who had been Miss Deaf Mississippi. She later married, so her *first runner up* took over as Miss Deaf America. Her name was Pam Young.

In 1976, Miss Deaf Maryland, Susan Davidoff, won the pageant. In 1978, Jackie Roth won (she too was replaced by the runner up, Debra Krause). In 1980, Mary Beth Barber, Miss Deaf New York, was crowned Miss Deaf America at the 100th Anniversary of the NAD.

Throughout the United States, deaf women compete in *local* pageants. The winners of the local pageants eventually compete in the national contest for the title of Miss Deaf America.

Vocabulary

pageant—N—a display, a parade, a theatrical exhibition

competed—V—tried to win

first runner up—N—second place winner

local—ADJ—small area near where you live

Captioned Television

Television was invented in the 1940s, and by the 1950s many American families owned television sets. During television's first 20 years, deaf people missed most of the fun. They could not hear what was being said and had to guess.

Malcolm J. Norwood

Deaf people who watched television enjoyed sports and action shows, but they were disappointed with other programs. If there was a lot of dialogue, deaf viewers missed the plot. Even the most skilled lipreaders could only catch part of the talking said. This frustrated many deaf people.

In the late 1960s, a man started experimenting. Malcolm Norwood thought that deaf people *could* enjoy television. He wanted to develop captions for the programs. Norwood worked for the federal government's Media Services and Captioned Films Division at the Bureau of Education of the Handicapped.

Norwood *surveyed* many hearing Americans. He wanted to see how they felt about seeing captions on the television screen. Too many people were against the idea. Norwood realized he had to develop another way of captioning—one that would not bother hearing people.

In October of 1971, Norwood's office signed a contract with WGBH-TV, a public television station in Boston. WGBH was hired to experiment with captions. They agreed to make a captioned television program for Norwood. That program was made. It was shown on television and at a special convention.

The type of captions made by WGBH could be seen on any television. No special equipment was needed. These were called "open captions."

Later, a new machine was invented. This *device* was made to send signals on a special part of the television picture. The signals could be captions. If a family had another kind of machine in their home, then the captions (or signals) would appear on their television screen. Without the machine, no captions would be seen. That special machine is called a decoder. It receives the signals transmitted from the television station. Captions that require a decoder are called "closed captions."

Vocabulary

surveyed—V—questioned
device—N—machine

The Caption Center at WGBH-TV

On December 3, 1973, WGBH-TV began broadcasting news with captions for deaf people. The captions were "open" and could be seen on any television set. No decoder was required to see the captioned news. Because of the success of this program, the Caption Center was established at WGBH-TV.

Each weekday evening, The Caption Center worked on their half hour program. They took the ABC Evening News, added captions and other information of interest to deaf people, and *rebroadcast* the program. The Captioned ABC News was shown every night at 11 p.m. on stations all over the U.S.

It was a big job to caption the ABC News. The staff at WGBH *taped* the show at 6:30 p.m. when it was shown on television without captions. Then they developed the *text*. They changed the language to fit the caption space and then added the printed text to the film.

The Caption Center has captioned many television programs since 1973 and continues captioning today.

National Captioning Institute

In 1976, the Federal Communications Commission, FCC, agreed to save part of the television picture for captioning. That part is called Line 21. It refers to a horizontal line near the bottom of the picture. That same year, the National Captioning Institute was founded to make more captioned television shows.

Sears, Roebuck and Co. agreed to make and sell the device needed to see captions. Their "decoder" is now used to watch programs that are closed captioned. It can be connected to any television set.

Three television networks—PBS, NBC, and ABC—agreed to show captioned programs. The first year of closed captioned television was 1980. Since that time, many different programs have been closed captioned. It took a long time, but deaf people can finally share the fun of television!

Deaf Awareness Programs

In the 1970s, many people worked hard to "raise *consciousness*" about deafness. Their goal was to end myths about deaf people. Some people still believed the *myths* that deaf people were not smart. The term "deaf and dumb" reflects the need for awareness.

Colorado had one of the first Deaf Awareness Weeks in 1972. It was very successful, and other states copied the idea. By 1975, there had been Deaf Awareness Weeks all over the nation.

At one high school, teachers and students volunteered to be deaf for a day. They put ear plugs in their ears.

Libraries participated in Deaf Awareness activities, too. Alice Hagemeyer *initiated* a Deaf Awareness Week at the Martin Luther King Memorial Library in Washington, D.C. That program included lectures by deaf people. Other libraries set up similar programs. All of them helped increase hearing people's awareness of deafness.

Deaf Awareness activities did a lot to help deaf people. Hearing people realized that deaf people were not different or stupid. Deaf people learned about services available to them. The plan to increase awareness worked!

Hearing Ear Dogs

In 1974, a deaf woman's dog died. The woman was very upset and worried because the dog "was her ears." Whenever there was a knock on her door, the dog would respond. The woman contacted the Society for Prevention of Cruelty to Animals, and they replaced her dog.

Two years later the Society sent six more dogs to live with deaf people. All of the six dogs had been trained to be "the ears" of their owners. These dogs were the first trained Hearing Ear Dogs.

Hearing Ear Dogs perform many *tasks*. They respond to knocks at the door, babies crying, telephones ringing, smoke detector alarms, etc.

The training program for Hearing Ear Dogs is now located in Englewood, Colorado, and is run by the American Humane Association.

Public Law 94-142

On November 29, 1975, President Gerald Ford signed a new law. It was *enacted* during the 94th session of Congress and is known as Public Law 94-142. It is also known by another name: the Education for all Handicapped Children Act of 1975.

PL 94-142 was a very important piece of *legislation.* It changed the responsibilities of local, state, and federal governments. They all had a new role in the education of handicapped children.

PL 94-142 requires parent involvement in their child's education. Parents' opinions have to be heard before a school makes a decision about classes. If parents do not like what a school plans to do for their son or daughter, they can *veto* it. For example, parents can request an oral or signing class for a deaf child.

The educational plan developed for each child is called an IEP, Individual Educational Plan. Children who are not handicapped do not have IEPs.

Some people think that PL 94-142 is a good law, and some people dislike it. For some deaf children, the law is bad. Many towns want to keep deaf children in local schools and *"mainstream"* them with hearing children. Some people believe this is the best education for a deaf child; some think it is better to send a deaf child to a school for deaf students.

In the future, many people will study this law. They will see how well students have done in school and decisions will be made about Public Law 94-142.

Deaf Ph.D.'s

The highest degree a person can earn through a university is a Ph.D. It takes years of study and work to earn and is very *prestigious.*

The earliest known deaf Ph.D. was Gideon Moore. He was born hearing but lost his hearing *progressively.* He graduated from Yale University in 1861 and then studied philosophy and chemistry at Heidelberg University in Germany. He earned his doctorate with highest honors! When Moore returned to the United States, he became a very successful chemist.

Edwin Nies became the second deaf person to earn a doctorate. He attended Lexington School for the Deaf in New York and graduated from Gallaudet College in 1911. He earned a dental degree (Doctor of Dental Surgery—D.D.S. degree) from the University of Pennsylvania Dental School in 1914. He was a dentist for many years and later became an Episcopal minister.

By 1974, 23 deaf Americans had earned doctoral degrees. Since that time, many more have joined the *ranks* of deaf Ph.D.'s. Some of the well known hearing-impaired people who have earned doctoral degrees are: James Marsters, dentistry; Richard Thompson, psychology; Joseph Parkinson, W.S. Smith, Sheila Conlon-Mentkowski and Lowell Myers, law; Raphael Price, medicine; and many others.

The White House Conference

The White House Conference on Handicapped Individuals met in Washington, D.C., for one week in 1977. The purpose of the conference was to *assess* problems and strengths of disabled Americans. After assessing strengths and weaknesses, the participants made recommendations to the President. Those recommendations could make people more understanding of all handicapped people. The recommendations would *enable* handicapped individuals to "live their lives independently with *dignity,* and with full participation in community life to the *greatest degree* possible." *Nearly* 3,000 people participated in the conference, and it was a great success.

Approximately 800 of the delegates to the conference were disabled. They came from all over the country. They represented the disabled population of the United States—35 million Americans!

Of the 800 delegates, 50 were deaf, and 28 *alternates* were deaf. Don Pettingill, a deaf man, was a *liaison* for the deaf participants.

At the end of his speech to the Conference, President Jimmy Carter signed, "God Bless You."

Don Pettingill

Chapter 11

The Ear and Deafness

The Ear: Outer and Middle

The ear is *comprised* of three main areas: the outer ear, middle ear, and inner ear. Each of these has different *structures*, different *functions*, and different problems.

The outer ear begins with the *pinna*. The pinna is easy to see because it is on the outside of the head. It is made of *cartilage* and helps to gather and localize sound. In animals, the pinna can move and tells them where sounds are. People do not have moveable pinnas, so they do not *localize* sound as much. The *auditory canal* begins at a small opening in the pinna and ends at the eardrum. It is a long, narrow tube which goes inside the head. Its function is to *direct* sound to the middle ear. If the auditory canal is blocked, sounds will be quieter and difficult to hear.

The middle ear begins at the *eardrum*. This thin piece of *tissue* covers the end of the auditory canal. When sounds travel through the auditory canal and reach the eardrum, it *vibrates*.

On the other side of the eardrum, there are three tiny bones. They are the smallest bones in the human body and are connected to each other. They are the *ossicles*, and they make the *ossicular chain*. The movement of the eardrum makes the first bone in the chain vibrate. This bone is the *malleus*, and it is the largest of the three ossicles. When the malleus vibrates, it makes the rest of the chain move. First the malleus, next the *incus*, and finally the *stapes*. Each bone's vibration makes the next bone move. If one of the ossicles is missing or broken, vibration stops. Damage to the ossicular chain can cause a hearing loss.

People who have a problem in the outer or middle ear have a *conductive* hearing loss. Conductive losses can usually be helped with hearing aids. Sometimes, *surgery* can correct the problem. Conductive losses can be caused by many problems such as: too much wax in the auditory canal, a *perforated* eardrum, an infection in the middle ear, or a broken bone in the ossicular chain.

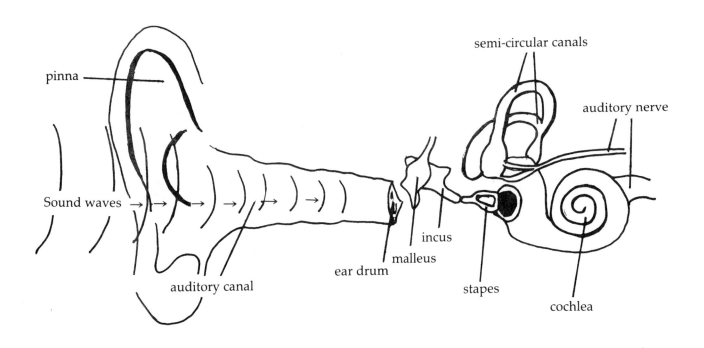

Diagram labels:

pinna

Sound waves →

auditory canal

ear drum

malleus

incus

semi-circular canals

auditory nerve

stapes

cochlea

Vocabulary

comprised—V—made up of; formed by

structures—N—parts; organs

functions—N—responsibilities; jobs

cartilage—N—a very thick, elastic kind of tissue; a flexible bone-like material

localize—V—identify where something comes from

direct—V—guide; assist

tissue—N—cells of the body

vibrate—V—to move very quickly; to shake

surgery—N—an operation by doctors

perforated—ADJ—having a hole through

The Ear: Inner

The inner ear has two main structures: the *semi-circular canals* and the *cochlea.* The *canals* are responsible for balance and the cochlea for hearing. Some diseases, like meningitis, can damage the *entire* inner ear. This is why some deaf people have balance *disorders.*

Inside the semi-circular canals is a special *fluid*. As the body moves, the fluid moves. This process maintains balance. When there are problems in the semi-circular canals, the person will have problems with balance and *equilibrium.*

The cochlea is the most *crucial* structure for hearing. It is very complex and *irreplaceable.* If people are born without a cochlea or with a damaged cochlea, they will have a permanent hearing loss. Scientists are experimenting with "cochlear implants"—*artificial* devices that replace damaged cochleas. Some people are trying to find ways to repair cochleas, but so far they have not succeeded. Cochlear implants help, but people who have them still do not regain normal hearing.

The cochlea is very important because it is where sound is sent to the brain. It has tiny nerves, *hair cells,* which are *stimulated* by fluid. When the middle ear vibrations reach the inner ear, the fluid moves. It touches the hair cells. The hair cells are very sensitive to fluid, and they send messages to the *auditory nerve.* This is a special nerve which connects the hair cells and the brain. The auditory nerve sends the message to the brain, and the brain *perceives* the sound.

Hearing aids are not a cure for cochlear damage. They are helpful, but will not solve the person's hearing problem. Doctors cannot operate on the hair cells, auditory nerve, or cochlea. When the eardrum is injured, it can grow back, but the cochlea cannot. Nerves do not grow back when they are hurt. Damage to the hair cells, auditory nerve, or cochlea is permanent. This type of hearing loss is a sensory-neural loss.

Most people who are profoundly deaf have a sensory-neural hearing loss. Although hearing aids help, they will never *restore* normal hearing to a person with a damaged cochlea or auditory nerve or with a missing cochlea.

Vocabulary

canals—N—tubes; tunnels
entire—ADJ—total; all parts
disorders—N—dysfunction; problems
fluid—N—liquid
equilibrium—N—keeping upright without dizziness; keeping balance
crucial—ADJ—necessary and important
irreplaceable—ADJ—cannot be replaced
artificial—ADJ—made by man; not natural
stimulated—V—activated; set into motion
perceives—V—receives and understands; recognizes
restore—V—bring back

Causes of Hearing Impairment

People can become hearing impaired at any age—before they are born, as infants, during childhood, or as adults. Each *age of onset* has a different name and may have different causes.

Prenatal deafness means that a baby is born deaf. There are several reasons why this can happen. If parents are deaf, they may have a deaf baby. This does not happen very often, though. There are also *genes* related to deafness that hearing parents can pass on to their child. Genes control the way we look and all of our *characteristics.* Even if parents are hearing, they may have genes for hearing impairments. If the baby gets these genes from hearing parents, it can be born deaf.

One of the most common types of prenatal deafness is caused by a disease. *Rubella* (German measles) is an illness that a pregnanat woman can get. She might not even realize that she has it. Unfortunately, the unborn baby can have terrible problems from *maternal* rubella. It can cause the baby to have eye problems, heart *defects,* learning disabilities, and deafness. It is especially bad if the woman has the disease when she is less than three months pregnant. During the 1960s, there was an *epidemic* of rubella, and thousands of children were affected. Many of them were born deaf.

Other prenatal causes of deafness can include: accidents; medicine or drugs that the mother takes; illnesses; and genetic *syndromes.* Genetic syndromes are a group of characteristics that a child inherits from its parents. There are two very common types of genetic syndromes related to deafness. One is *Waardenburg's Syndrome.* Its characteristics are very obvious. The person may have pigment disorders: a streak of white hair; two different color eyes; or streaks of white in a man's beard. Most residential schools have children with these characteristics. It is possible to have the physical traits of Waardenburg's Syndrome but not be deaf.

Usher's Syndrome is also fairly common. Children with Usher's Syndrome are born with a hearing loss and later lose their vision. The first symptoms of this genetic syndrome occur at night. A person with Usher's Syndrome will experience problems seeing well at night. Later, they will lose their *peripheral* vision and see only within a tunnel area in front of them. This is called "tunnel vision." Persons may eventually lose more and more of their vision and become blind or partially blind. If you notice that a deaf person does not see you when you are at his side, he may have this problem. The best way to communicate with a person who has Usher's Syndrome is to stand directly in front and to sign clearly. If you know someone who has Usher's Syndrome, try to be supportive and helpful.

Vocabulary

"age of onset"—age when the problem begins

prenatal—ADJ—before birth

genes—N—parts of the cell which control our development

characteristics—N—traits

maternal—ADJ—characteristic of a mother

defects—N—mistakes; irregularities

epidemic—N—a situation when many people become ill from one disease

syndrome—N—a combination of characteristics

peripheral—ADJ—outermost; along the periphery

Causes of Hearing Loss: In Infancy

*I*nfants can also lose their hearing. If there is a problem during birth, brain damage can result. Sometimes, a baby is not in the right position to be born. A doctor has to move the baby inside the mother. The doctor might use *forceps* to do this. The forceps are used on the baby's head, and they sometimes push on the brain. This can cause brain damage and may even *permanently* damage the child. When this happens, the child can be born mentally retarded or deaf.

Although pregnancy is supposed to last for nine months, babies are sometimes born early. If this happens, and the baby is very tiny, it is called a *premature* birth. Premature babies can have many problems because their bodies are too small or not fully developed. One problem that can happen is related to the *respiratory system*. If the respiratory system is not strong enough, the baby can stop breathing. The brain needs oxygen, and if the baby stops breathing, the brain doesn't get the oxygen it needs. The brain can be hurt, and the baby can be deaf or mentally retarded.

Another *complication* which can occur to a newborn baby is related to the blood. If the baby and its mother have different blood types, there can be many problems. Everyone has a different blood type: some people are O, some A positive, some B negative, or AB + or AB − . There are many different combinations of letters and positive or negative. When the mother has a negative type and the baby has a positive type, a situation called *incompatibility* occurs. This means that the baby's blood and the mother's blood do not get along. They both become very sick from this. When the baby is born, all of its blood has to be removed, and new blood added. This *transfusion* of blood saves the baby's life. If the baby's blood conflicts with its mother's there can be damage even before the transfusion. It can be deaf. Many babies do not even *survive* when there is a blood incompatibility problem. Fortunately, the incompatibility of baby's and mother's blood can be controlled today. There are new medicines doctors use to solve the problem. Not many babies have to go through such a terrible experience any more.

The problems that a child has from an early age of onset are related to language. If the baby loses its hearing before it learns to talk, it will not know a language. Losing hearing before age three is called *prelingual* deafness. This means the child became deaf before it learned a language. When a child knows how to talk and then loses its hearing, usually after age three, it is called *postlingual* deafness, which means after language has been learned.

Vocabulary

infants—N—very young babies; newborns

forceps—N—very large tweezers

permanently—ADV—forever; not temporary

premature—ADJ—before maturity; early (birth)

respiratory system—N—the part of the body responsible for breathing

complication—N—serious problem

incompatibility—N—a conflict; not getting along well

transfusion—N—removal of blood then replacing it with new blood

survive—V—live

prelingual—ADJ—before learning or understanding language

postlingual—ADJ—after learning or understanding language

Chapter 12

The World of Sports

(Deaf Heritage, pp. 271–316)

Football

Football became a *major* sport in schools for the deaf around the turn of the century. Gallaudet College students played football even earlier, during the 1880s. Five members of Gallaudet's first team in 1883 later became NAD presidents: Thomas Francis Fox, George W. Veditz, Olof Hanson, James L. Smith, and James Cloud.

Art Kruger, sports editor of *The Deaf American*, *estimates* that there have been over 1,000 football games between schools for the deaf. The first game between two deaf schools was in 1903. It was between the North Carolina School for the Deaf and the Tennessee School for the Deaf. Tennessee won. The second *interscholastic* contest was in 1920 with the Kansas and Missouri schools for the deaf competing. That game was won by Kansas.

In 1976, the first international football game was played. The teams in that match were from the Michigan School and the Ontario (Canada) School for the Deaf. Michigan won, 74–12.

A few deaf athletes have played *professional* football. In the 1920s, Joe Allen played for a tough Ohio team, the Sandusky Maroons. In the 1930s, Bilbo Monaghan played for a *pro* team in Memphis, Tennessee. His coach learned sign language so they could communicate. In the late 1960s, Ray Parks and Edward Gobble played for the Frederick Falcons, a semi-pro team. William Zachariasen was also a member of the Frederick Falcons. In 1973, Bonnie Sloan was drafted by the St. Louis Cardinals and was the starting *tackle* during his first season. Unfortunately, he injured his right knee and was not able to *regain* his starting position.

The Goodyear Silents

The Goodyear Silents was a semi-professional football team in Akron, Ohio. Graduates of Gallaudet College and schools for the deaf played for the team. It was organized in

Art Kruger, 1949

Lenny Meyer

The American Athletic Association of the Deaf

The American Athletic Association of the Deaf, AAAD, is composed of seven *regions*. It has over 150 participating clubs. It was the first national deaf organization to *prohibit* racial discrimination. Basketball tournaments are held annually in different parts of the country. The AAAD also has an annual softball tourney.

The AAAD was organized for six main reasons: to encourage competition among clubs and have uniform rules; to provide social activities for members and their friends; to help other regional athletic associations; to conduct an annual basketball tournament; to improve and maintain *standards* of athletic competition; and to help the United States team in international competition.

In 1952, the AAAD established a Hall of Fame. This recognizes outstanding deaf athletes, coaches, and sports leaders.

1916 and had a very successful record. In 1917, the team won eight of 10 games and became the Central Ohio Champs. The team was *undefeated* in 1918 and lost only one game in 1919. In 1920, the Silents lost one game, and the next year lost two, tied one, and won nine. From 1919–1922, their record was 39 wins, three losses, and three ties.

After 1922, the team could not find enough players, and by 1925 the team ended.

World Games for the Deaf

The International Games for the Deaf were organized in Paris, France, in 1924. At that time, American athletes did not compete. They entered the Games in 1935 when S. Robey Burns brought two athletes to the Games. He was a coach at the Illinois School for the Deaf.

The name for the Games changed to "The World Games for the Deaf" later. By 1957, there were 40 American athletes participating, and the American Athletic Association of the Deaf became involved in organizing the American team.

In 1965, America hosted the World Games for the Deaf in Washington, D.C. That year, the Games were organized, planned, and run by deaf people.

Vocabulary

major—ADJ—important; featured

estimates—V—gives an approximate number

interscholastic—ADJ—between two schools

professional—ADJ—receiving a salary for; not a volunteer; not amateur

"pro"—professional

tackle—N—one of the positions on a football team

regain—V—get back

undefeated—ADJ—without any defeats; without a loss

regions—N—geographic areas; parts of the country

prohibit—V—ban; forbid

standards—N—rules

Chapter 13

NAD's First Hundred Years 1880–1980

Years 1880–1920

1880—National Convention of Deaf-Mutes held in Cincinnati, Ohio, with 143 participants from 21 states.

1883—Second NAD convention held in New York City with 174 participants from 18 states; members decided to raise money for a statue in honor of Thomas Hopkins Gallaudet.

1887—$13,000 raised for the Gallaudet memorial statue.

1889—Third convention of the NAD held in Washington, D.C.

—The statue of Gallaudet and Alice Cogswell was *unveiled* on the campus of the National Deaf-Mute College.

—The members of the association *object* to discrimination in *Civil Service* and referring to schools for the deaf as "asylums."

1893—Fourth convention held in Chicago.

1896—Fifth convention held in Philadelphia.

—Julia Foley became first woman elected to NAD Board.

1899—Sixth convention in St. Paul, Minnesota.

—NAD formally supports the Combined System of educating deaf children.

1900—NAD incorporated in Washington, D.C.

1904—Seventh convention in St. Louis, Missouri.

—Members expressed concerns about trends in education of the deaf and voted to publish and *circulate* information about the deaf and deafness to educators, legislators, parents, and others.

—Passed a resolution requesting more vocational training for deaf students.

—Formally recommended establishing schools for black deaf children.

1907—Eighth convention in Norfolk, Virginia.

—Committee established to meet with the Civil Service Commission about discrimination against deaf workers.

1910—Ninth convention held at Colorado Springs, Colorado, with 520 participants.

—President William Taft informed the NAD he had told the Civil Service Commission to remove all discrimination against the deaf.

—Deaf people were urged to vote for Taft.

1913—Tenth convention held in Cleveland, Ohio.

—NAD unsuccessful in convincing Nebraska State legislature to *repeal* law requiring the use of oral methods to teach deaf students.

1915—Eleventh convention held in San Francisco, California.

—NAD continued fight against Nebraska oral law.

1917—Twelfth convention held in Hartford, Connecticut, to honor the *centennial* of the founding of the first permanent school for the deaf in the U.S.

—NAD raised money for three ambulances to help the French in World War I.

—Supported the idea of sending deaf children to school at an earlier age (usually, children started at age eight).

1920—Thirteenth convention held in Detroit, Michigan; 2,589 people participated in the convention.

Years 1921–1960

1923—Fourteenth convention held in Atlanta, Georgia.

1926—Fifteenth convention held in Washington, D.C.

—Members concerned about threats to driving rights.

1930—Sixteenth convention held in Buffalo, New York, during the fourth World Congress of the Deaf.

—NAD presented statue of Charles Michael de l'Epee (founder of the first free school for the deaf in the world) to Le Couteulx St. Mary's Institution for the Deaf in Buffalo.

1934—Seventeenth convention held in New York City.

1937—Eighteenth convention held in Chicago, Illinois.

—Members protested *discrimination* against the deaf by the Civilian Conservation Corps, Social Security Administration, and Works Progress Administration.

—President Roosevelt promised to increase his support for Civil Service jobs for deaf people.

1940—Nineteenth convention held in Los Angeles, California.

—NAD tried to obtain special services for deaf people in vocational rehabilitation, *criticized* "dumping" *slow* deaf *students* on residential schools and keeping the *bright students* for the oral schools.

1941–45—NAD established "Victory Fund" to help the U.S. during World War II and raised nearly $8,000.
    —NAD fought a St. Louis court case in which a deaf man lost his driver's license because he could not hear.
    —NAD battled the New York Legislature which required a doctor's approval before giving a driver's license to a deaf person.
1946—Twentieth convention held in Louisville, Kentucky.
1949—Twenty-First convention held in Cleveland, Ohio.
    —NAD officials said they needed a permanent home office and a full-time staff.
    —NAD helped state associations for the deaf in Michigan, Ohio, Texas, and Virginia fight for *reforms* in education and *construction* of new schools.
    —Assisted deaf workers to fight discrimination by the Civil Service.
    —Started a movement to get two professional baseball players placed in the Hall of Fame (both players, William Hoy and Luther Taylor were deaf).
1950—First home office of the NAD opened in Chicago.
1953—Twenty-second convention held in Austin, Texas.
    —NAD attacked a South Dakota newspaper proposing a *ban* on deaf drivers.
    —Fought a plan to replace the Kendall School in Washington, D.C., with an oral day school.
1953—Fought a proposal by New York's Senator Jacob Javits to give deaf people an extra $600 tax exemption.
1955—Twenty-third convention held in Cincinnati, Ohio.

Vocabulary

discrimination—N—treating people unfairly
criticized—V—made negative comments; said bad things about
"dumping"—abandoning; getting rid of something unwanted
slow students—N—students who are not very smart
bright students—N—smart students
reforms—N—improvements
construction—N—establishment; creation
ban—N—an order that prohibits something; a law against something
occupations—N—jobs; professions; careers
excessive—ADJ—too much
elimination—N—removal of someone or something

    —NAD received a grant of $17,200 to survey *occupations* among the deaf.
    —NAD supported a bill to Congress to provide captioned films for the deaf.
1956—NAD "reorganizational meeting" held at Missouri School for the Deaf in Fulton.
1957—Twenty-fourth convention held in St. Louis, Missouri.
    —NAD helped Georgia deaf get hearing test law for all drivers repealed.
    —NAD received an additional $30,000 grant to complete the survey on occupations.
1960—Twenty-fifth convention held in Dallas, Texas, under newly reorganized by-laws.
    —New membership drive for the NAD started.
    —NAD recommended that salaries

be increased for residential school teachers and counselors.

—Supported the Iowa Association of the Deaf in their fight against *excessive* use of the oral method and opposed the *elimination* of deaf teachers.

Years 1961–1980

1962—Twenty-seventh convention held in Washington, D.C.

—NAD began evaluating entertainment films for Captioned Films for the Deaf.

—*Circulation* of *The Silent Worker* (renamed *The Deaf American*) hit 2,400.

—Home Office of NAD moved to Washington, D.C.

1966—Twenty-eighth convention held in San Francisco.

—NAD voted to hire first full-time executive secretary.

—Frederick Schreiber appointed Executive Secretary.

—NAD developed *joint* workshop with Registry of Interpreters for the Deaf.

—Established a cultural program to encourage cultural activities among the deaf.

—NAD awarded first Distinguished Service Award to Boyce R. Williams.

1967—NAD awarded a grant of $75,000 from the Vocational Rehabilitation Administration to have an international *seminar* on research in vocational rehabilitation.

—Received another grant of $48,000 to develop a sign language program; Terrence O'Rourke hired to direct the sign language project.

—Provided legal help and raised $3,000 to help a deaf couple in California with their adoption case.

—Home Office doubled in size and moved to a new location.

1968—Twenty-ninth convention held in Las Vegas.

—NAD approved a 37½ hour work week for Home Office employees and added health insurance and life insurance to employees' benefits.

—Executive Secretary's salary increased to $17,000.

1969—NAD supported Congressional legislation establishing the National Technical Institute for the Deaf (NTID) and the Model Secondary School for the Deaf.

—Held first leadership workshop in Salt Lake City, Utah, to train deaf people in leadership techniques.

1970—Thirtieth convention held in Minneapolis, Minnesota.

—Circulation of *The Deaf American* reached 4,600.

Frederick C. Schreiber

—Home Office announced publication of a new book *A Basic Course in Manual Communication* by Terrence O'Rourke.

1971—Executive Board of NAD *purchased* Halex House in Silver Spring, Maryland, for $640,000.
—Circulation of *The Deaf American* reached 5,000.

1972—Thirty-first convention held in Miami Beach, Florida.
—Home Office began training deaf students "on-the-job."
—NAD published seven books and hired a full-time director for publications.
—NAD hired a librarian and started a library.
—Jr. NAD published *The Jr. Deaf American* and *Silent Voice*.

1973—300 persons attended opening of the NAD owned building, Halex House.

1974—Thirty-second convention held in Seattle, Washington.
—Junior NAD Director (Frank R. Turk) reported 79 Junior NAD chapters.
—Circulation of *The Deaf American* reached 6,500.

1976—Thirty-third convention held in Houston, Texas.
—NAD established NAD Legal Defense Fund.
—Began a joint project with Gallaudet College to sponsor regional leadership training programs for deaf Americans.

1977—Frederick Schreiber received honorary degree from Gallaudet College.

1978—Thirty-fourth convention held in Rochester, New York.
—NAD tried to have sign language taught in public schools and accepted as a second language in high schools and colleges.
—Concern expressed about "mainstreaming."
—NAD awarded Bernard Bragg $2,000 to advocate sign language around the world and to encourage deaf theatre.
—NAD opened Branch Office in Indianapolis, Indiana, and hired Gary Olsen as assistant director for State Affairs.

1979—NAD began publication of *The NAD Broadcaster* newspaper.
—Frederick Schreiber died in a New York Hospital.
—Albert T. Pimentel hired as executive director of the National Association of the Deaf.

1980—Centennial convention held in Cincinnati, Ohio.
—Maryland's Gertrude Galloway became first female president of the NAD.

Vocabulary

circulation—N—the number of issues distributed; subscribers
joint—ADJ—together; cooperative
seminar—N—educational workshop
purchased—V—bought

Prologue

Pages 1–2

Comprehension Questions

1. When did the Mary Augusta leave France?

2. What were the names of the two important passengers on the ship?

3. Why did Gallaudet go to Europe?

4. Did the owners of the school in England cooperate with Gallaudet?

5. How did Clerc and Gallaudet meet?

6. Why did Clerc move to America?

7. If Clerc turned down Gallaudet's invitation, do you think schools for the deaf would be different today? Explain your answer.

Matching

___Braidwood   a. A deaf girl who lived in Connecticut
___Clerc   b. the family name of English teachers of the deaf
___Gallaudet   c. the father of Gallaudet's first student
___Dr. Cogswell   d. a student-minister who became a teacher of the deaf
___Alice Cogswell   e. the first *deaf* teacher of the deaf in America

Follow-Up Activities for Students

1. Write an essay beginning with "If Clerc refused to come to America . . ."
2. Read pages xxi and xxii in *Deaf Heritage* and describe Clerc and Gallaudet from the pictures on page xxiii.
3. Discuss as a class the reason for erecting the statue at Gallaudet College which depicts Alice and Gallaudet. Who was the sculptor?

Chapter 1 Education of Deaf Children 1816–1851

Pages 3–4

Comprehension Questions

1. What school for the deaf opened in Hartford, Connecticut, in 1817?

2. Who established the Connecticut Asylum?

3. Why did John Jacobs ride his horse to Connecticut?

4. By the time Gallaudet died, how many schools for the deaf were there in America?

5. If you were Gallaudet, how would you feel about your many accomplishments?

6. Why should deaf people feel proud of Laurent Clerc?

7. Note the term used in the 1800s—*Deaf and Dumb*. Why was this name used? Is this name still used by most people today? Why or why not?

Matching

——Kentucky School for the Deaf

——John Jacobs

——Pennsylvania Institution

——American School for the Deaf

——American Asylum

——Connecticut Asylum for the Education and Instruction of Deaf and Dumb Persons

——New York Institution for the Instruction of the Deaf and Dumb

a. the original name of the American School for the Deaf

b. the second name given to the American School for the Deaf

c. the famous teacher from Kentucky who was trained in Connecticut

d. the first state-supported school for the deaf

e. the second school for the deaf in America

f. the school for the deaf that opened in 1820

g. the name used today for the school established by Clerc and Gallaudet

1. How many schools for the deaf opened between 1817 and 1851?

2. The names of some schools for the deaf have changed over the years. The American School for the Deaf used to have another name—The American Asylum. Why do you think the word "asylum" was changed?

3. Thomas H. Gallaudet died in 1851. Can you predict how his death changed schools for the deaf? Do you think there were changes? Describe your predictions.

Deaf Teachers

Pages 4–6

Comprehension Questions

1. Name three positive role models for deaf students in the 1800s.

2. Why were Amanda Johnson and Julius Carrett hired to teach in Texas?

3. Why did schools stop hiring deaf teachers? When did these changes occur?

4. Do you think there are enough deaf teachers today? Explain your answer.

5. Are there many black deaf teachers today? Are there any at your school?

6. Who are your role models?

7. How can you be a positive role model for younger deaf students?

Matching

___Laurent Clerc	a. the first male black deaf teacher
___Amanda Johnson	b. the first female black deaf teacher
___Julius Carrett	c. the first deaf teacher of the deaf in the U.S.
___13.6 percent	d. the percentage of deaf teachers in 1858
___40.8 percent	e. the percentage of deaf teachers today

The Civil War Years

Pages 6–7

Comprehension Questions

1. What name refers to the northern Army?

2. What name refers to the southern Army?

3. Why did some schools have to close during the Civil War?

4. How did John Jacobs keep his school open?

5. What did soldiers think when they heard the mooing cows?

Follow-Up Activities for Students

1. Refer to *Deaf Heritage,* p. 23, to read about the Tennessee School during the Civil War and why it is a National Landmark today.
2. Discuss the impact of the Civil War on deaf students. Was it fair that their education had to stop while the war was on?
3. Does being deaf unite everyone regardless of political feelings? How do students feel about this concept?
4. Investigate your school's status during the Civil War.

Sign Language Saves A Life

Pages 7–8

Comprehension Questions

1. Who captured Joshua and why?

2. Was Joshua really a spy?

3. Why did the officer order Joshua's release?

4. If the officer on horseback never arrived, what would have happened to Joshua?

5. How old was Joshua when he died?

6. How did Joshua's family feel about the officer?

7. Even though the officer and the Davis family were enemies, they became friends. How could this happen?

Time Line 1852–1866

Page 9

Comprehension Questions

1. How many new schools opened during this period of 14 years?

2. When and where did the first college for deaf students open?

3. Why did John Carlin and others use Laurent Clerc's name in a new society?

4. Do you know the current name for the National Deaf-Mute College?

5. Who signed the charter for the first college for deaf students?

Oral Education in America

Pages 8-9

Comprehension Questions

1. When did Engelsman move to New York City?

2. Where was Engelsman a teacher of the deaf?

3. What kind of teaching methods did Engelsman use?

4. Explain how the Clarke School for the Deaf was established.

5. Did Engelsman and Hubbard agree on methods of teaching the deaf? What was their method?

6. In your own words, explain what the quotation in the first paragraph of "Oral Education in America" means.

7. Did the American Asylum change its methods when oralism became popular?

Matching

___ Lexington School for the Deaf
___ Clarke School for the Deaf
___ American Asylum
___ Chelmsford, Massachusetts
___ Northampton, Massachusetts
___ Engelsman
___ Hubbard
___ "The German Method"

a. the second and present site of Hubbard's school
b. an oral teacher of the deaf who established the Lexington School for the Deaf
c. the pure oral school for the deaf in Northampton, Massachusetts
d. the first and original site of Hubbard's school
e. the name given to Heinicke's methods by deaf adults
f. a school which never became purely oral
g. a famous oral school for the deaf in New York City
h. the founder of the Clarke School for the Deaf

Time Line 1867–1880

Page 10

Comprehension Questions

1. How many oral schools opened during this period (judging from the schools' names)?

2. How many day schools opened during this period?

3. Do you think that new schools used sign language during this time? Why or why not?

4. What important group did Alexander Bell establish?

5. Two very important things happened in 1880. What were they?

6. After the Milan Conference in 1880, how do you think *deaf* teachers felt?

Chapter 2   1880: A Year to Remember

Pages 11–12

Comprehension Questions

1. What two important conventions took place in 1880 and where?

2. Which convention passed a resolution forbidding the use of signs with deaf students?

3. Who was Robert McGregor and why is he important to the National Association of the Deaf?

4. Do you think that 1880 was a good year for deaf people or a bad year? Why?

5. Who voted against the new resolution at the Milan Congress?

6. Who was the deaf delegate at the Milan Congress?

7. If the Milan Congress had not passed the rule about signing, how do you think deaf people would be taught today? Do you think that oral schools would have grown popular in America? Why or why not?

8. Why did deaf people feel the need for their own organization?

9. How old is the National Association of the Deaf today?

The Influence of Alexander Graham Bell

Pages 12–13

Comprehension Questions

1. What kinds of views did Alexander G. Bell have about deaf people marrying other deaf people?

2. Did Dr. Bell believe in separate schools for deaf children? Why or why not?

3. What do you think Bell meant by the term a deaf "race"?

4. Do *you* think most people who are deaf prefer socializing with deaf or hearing friends? Why?

5. Do you agree with Dr. Bell's idea to have a law prohibiting deaf people from intermarrying? Explain your answer.

6. Why did Bell drop his idea of the intermarriage law?

More About Alexander Graham Bell

Pages 13–14

Comprehension Questions

1. Who was Mabel Hubbard?

2. The father and husband of Mabel Hubbard both believed in teaching deaf children one way— were they advocates of signing or oralism?

3. Why did George Veditz say deaf people feared Bell?

4. Did the president of the National Deaf-Mute College share Bell's ideas?

5. What system of communication was used by Edward Miner Gallaudet's students at the National Deaf-Mute College?

6. Current research shows Bell may have been wrong about one thing. Bell said that deaf children who had signing deaf parents would not have good English skills. How did this research show Bell's theory may be wrong?

7. How do *you* feel about Bell using only speech with his wife, even though he knew sign language?

Time Line—1880–1900

Page 15

Comprehension Questions

1. How many state schools opened during 1880–1900? How many oral schools?

2. Do you think that deaf education grew during this period of time? Why or why not?

3. There was a big "surge" or increase in the number of oral schools during this time. Do you think deaf teachers were hired more or less with the new oral schools? Why or why not?

Follow-Up Activities for Students Based on Chapters 1 and 2

1. Try to locate an older, preferably elderly, deaf person. The older person should be interviewed about "the old days," so that students can get a feel for life as a deaf person in the early part of this century.

2. Interview the president or an officer of their state association of the deaf to find out what goals are presently being addressed by the organization.

3. Conduct an historical investigation of your school, including:
    a. date and place of founding.
    b. names of founders and status (deaf or hearing).
    c. original name of school and subsequent name changes.
    d. names of members of first graduating class.
    e. a flow chart showing growth or decrease in school/staff population.
    f. philosophical history of the school through the years—oral/manual.
    g. the names of all deaf teachers/administrators to work at the school since its founding.

4. Do independent projects on any of the following:
    a. history of the NAD.
    b. history of the Alexander G. Bell Association.

c. history of the Volta Bureau.
d. biography of Alexander Graham Bell.
e. biography of Laurent Clerc.
f. biography of Thomas H. or Edward Miner Gallaudet.
g. comparative study of French Sign Language and American Sign Language.

5. Do a large United States map using push-pins to locate all of the schools for the deaf. The pins could be color-coded to show:
a. decade of founding.
b. philosophical status (manual or oral).
c. founded by deaf or hearing educators.

Chapter 3　　　Biographical Information
McGregor, Hodgson, Booth

Pages 16–17

Comprehension Questions

1. What did the three men, Hodgson, Booth, and McGregor, all have in common?

2. Who was the first president of the NAD?

3. Who was the second president?

4. Why was *The Deaf Mutes' Journal* important to the NAD?

5. Who was nominated for the presidency of the NAD and declined?

6. When was the NAD established?

7. Which of the three men did not become deaf until the age of 18?

Biographical Information
Turner, Logan

Pages 17–18

Comprehension Questions

1. When Job Turner was a child, where did he attend school? Why?

2. Who was Turner's boss at the Virginia School for the Deaf?

3. Was Mr. Tyler deaf or hearing?

4. After Mrs. Turner died, what did Job decide to do with the rest of his life?

5. Were many deaf people ministers in the 1870s? Name two.

6. Describe Job Turner's life using four different adjectives.

7. What book made James Logan famous?

8. What was *The Raindrop* about?

9. Who else wrote the book with Mr. Logan?

10. Why did the magazine end?

11. Where did James Logan and George Teegarden work, and what were their jobs?

Follow-Up Activities for Students

1. Read *Deaf Heritage* pp. 59–69 for more information about the people just described.
2. Look at copies of *The Raindrop* to see the work of Teegarden and Logan.
3. Make a class time-line listing all of the presidents of the NAD since its inception.
4. Develop your own Raindrop edition with original poetry and stories.

Biographical Information
Flournoy

Page 19

Comprehension Questions

1. Why did some people disagree with John Flournoy's unique idea?

2. What was a "Deaf-Mute Colony"?

3. How did Edmund Booth feel about a separate community for deaf people?

4. Do you think that Flournoy would like mainstreaming if he were alive today? Why or why not?

5. What was Flournoy's dream that became reality?

6. What state school for the deaf did Flournoy help to found?

Biographical Information
Bridgman

Page 19

Comprehension Questions

1. Why is Laura Bridgman remembered today?

2. Who taught Laura when she was a student at Perkins?

3. What famous author wrote about Laura's school in a book?

4. Do people still read Charles Dickens' books and stories today? How do you know?

5. How do you think Laura and Charles Dickens communicated?

6. Do you think Laura was smart? Why?

Follow-Up Activities for Students

1. Research the Perkins School for the Blind in class and report on some of its well known graduates. (Helen Keller, Tom Sullivan . . .)
2. As a class, experience a "Trust-Walk" to understand what life is like for a deaf-blind person.
3. Interview a person with Usher's Syndrome to find out how he or she feels about progressive blindness.
4. Read *If You Could See What I Hear*, an autobiography of a blind man, Tom Sullivan.
5. Read and discuss any articles or books available about Helen Keller.

Biographical Information
Ballin

Page 20

Comprehension Questions

1. Where was David Ballin born?

2. What was David's profession?

3. Who was David Ballin's famous son?

4. What kinds of ideas did Albert have about residential schools?

5. What controversial person was Albert's close friend?

6. Where did Ballin and Bell first meet?

7. How did Alexander G. Bell feel about using signs in schools?

8. Where did Albert learn to paint?

9. What is the name of the book authored by Albert Ballin?

Biographical Information
Bloch

Pages 20–21

Comprehension Questions

1. In what country was David Bloch born and raised?

2. Where was he sent by the Nazis?

3. Why do you think that David Bloch was sent to a concentration camp?

4. After the war, where did he move?

5. When did Bloch come to America and with whom?

6. Why is David Bloch famous today?

Biographical Information
O'Neil

Page 21

Comprehension Questions

1. List four of the stunts that Kitty has performed.

2. Why was Kitty O'Neil at the 1964 Olympics?

3. In what nation were the 1964 Olympics?

4. How did Kitty O'Neil get her nicknames? Explain.

5. Did Kitty go to schools for the deaf when she was growing up?

6. Have you ever seen a stunt performed on television? Why is it important that other people do not try stunts—only stuntsmen and stuntswomen?

Biographical Information
Smith

Pages 21–22

Comprehension Questions

1. What made Linwood Smith a good role model for black deaf children?

2. How old was Smith when he died? How did he die?

3. What was Smith's legacy?

Follow-Up Activities for Students

1. Look up publications by Linwood Smith in the journals mentioned above.
2. Obtain copies of *Silence, Love, and Kids I Know*, read and discuss it.
3. Read *Black and Deaf in America* by Ernest Hairston and Linwood Smith.

Chapter 4   The National Fraternal Society of the Deaf

Pages 23–24

Comprehension Questions

1. Why was the 1898 meeting held and by whom?

2. When was the Fraternal Society of the Deaf established?

3. What do the letters N.F.S.D. represent?

4. Who was Peter Hellers?

5. List five ways that an insurance company can help people.

6. Why do you think deaf people could not get insurance in the past?

7. What are some of the NFSD's other contributions to the deaf community?

8. Why does the last line say that the NFSD is providing insurance for deaf youth? What do you think this line means?

Follow-up Activities for Students

1. Read pp. 157–163 in *Deaf Heritage* for more information about NFSD.
2. Interview parents to find out what kinds of insurance the family has.
3. Investigate local restrictions for deaf drivers. Are there any and how do students feel about them?
4. Interview the local NFSD division president to obtain a local chapter history.
5. Find out if any students from your school have been awarded NFSD scholarships or Savings Bonds. What are their names?

Homes for the Aged and Infirm Deaf

Pages 24–25

Comprehension Questions

1. When did interest grow for setting up homes for deaf senior citizens?

2. How was Thomas H. Gallaudet's son involved in this?

3. What home for elderly deaf people is run by Eddy Laird?

4. Which home closed in 1940 and why?

5. Why was the Indiana home built on the site of a farm?

Follow-up Activities for Students

1. Visit a local nursing home to see if there are any deaf residents. If so, with whom do they interact?
2. Contact the Senior Citizens Section of the NAD in their area and research the group's history.
3. Write an essay about life as an elderly deaf person prior to 1900. What communication problems might exist for an old deaf person? Where would an elderly deaf person live without a home for aged deaf?

Preserving Sign Language

Page 25

Comprehension Questions

1. Why did the NAD establish the Motion Pictures Committee?

2. Why is Roy Stewart remembered today?

3. Why were so many films lost?

4. What kind of films did the Motion Picture Committee make and why?

5. Are the original films still available today? If not, how can they be seen?

Follow-Up Activities for Students

If it is possible, the class should see the videotapes and analyze the signs. Have they changed in any way? Can they be understood? A discussion of changes in language and vocabulary can follow—slang, vocabulary used by each generation, etc.

Deaf Pilots

Page 26

Comprehension Questions

1. Who was the first person to make a transatlantic plane trip?

2. Who was the deaf woman who became a pilot in 1928?

3. How did Nellie use her plane to earn money?

4. Who was Edward Payne?

Follow-Up Activities for Students

1. For those interested in learning more about flying, suggested topics for reading include:
   a. Amelia Earhart
   b. Charles Lindbergh
   c. World War I flying aces
   d. World War II flying aces
   e. astronauts.
2. Students can read more about the deaf aviators in *Deaf Heritage*, page 201.

Time Line—1900–1940

Page 27

Comprehension Questions and Follow-Up Activities

1. In 1912, the teacher training program at Gallaudet College was renamed. What was the new name, and why do you think it was changed? If you do not understand the words in the new name, ask your teacher to explain them to you.

2. During the period of time described in this chapter, 1900–1940, many changes occurred in the world. Make a time line of world events.

3. It seems that this 40 year period was not very good for deaf people. Which very strong leader of the deaf died? Do you think this helped the "cause" of deaf people?

4. How many schools opened during this period? Which schools opened?

Chapter 5   The Attack on Pearl Harbor

Page 28

Comprehension Questions

1. Where is Pearl Harbor?

2. In what state is Diamond Head School for the Deaf?

3. When was the Japanese attack on Pearl Harbor?

4. How did Bill Sugiyama know something was wrong?

5. How did the attack change life at the school for the deaf in Oahu?

Doing One's Share

Pages 29–30

Comprehension Questions

1. Describe ways that deaf Americans helped the country during World War II.

2. What happened to Japanese Americans during the war and why?

The *U.S.S. Thomas Hopkins Gallaudet*

Pages 30–31

Comprehension Questions

1. When was the *Thomas Hopkins Gallaudet* ship completed?

2. Who built the ship?

3. What were the five other names used for the *Thomas Hopkins Gallaudet?*

4. When did the Samuel S. run aground and what was the result?

5. Is the *Samuel S.* still sailing today?

The Post-War Years

Page 31

Comprehension Questions

1. Were there many deaf teachers in the post-World War II years?

2. Which schools had many deaf teachers?

3. What did the Mississippi Association of the Deaf do to help deaf children?

4. Before the new Mississippi laws, what do you think happened to deaf children who did not lipread or speak well? How did the new law help them?

The Best Survey

Pages 32–33

Comprehension Questions

1. Before Dr. Best was hired to study Gallaudet, what was the college like?

2. What did President Elstad tell alumni at their 20th reunion?

3. Did Elstad's hopes come true?

4. How did people react to Best's ideas?

5. Who was Gallagher, and why was he hired by the government?

6. What did Gallagher suggest the government do?

7. Did Gallagher help or hurt Gallaudet College? How?

Captioned Films for the Deaf

Pages 33–34

Comprehension Questions

1. Who was the first person to splice films and add captions?

2. Was the person in question #1 deaf or hearing?

3. What problems did Mr. Romero face with his project?

4. Which three men worked on captioning and founded Captioned Films for the Deaf in 1950?

5. When the federal organization was established by an act of Congress, what was it called?

6. What federal agency funded the captioning? Which agency ran the captioning project?

7. How much money had been spent by 1970 on captioning films for deaf people?

Follow-up Activities for Students

Teachers should show several types of captioned films and offer them as examples of captioning technique: filmstrips, captioned entertainment films, captioned educational films, captioned TV with closed captions (simultaneous and regular), and, if available, foreign films with subtitles. Discussion can follow regarding which type the students understand most and least and why.

Time Line—1940–1960

Page 34

Comprehension Questions

1. How many schools for the deaf opened during this 20-year period?

2. Which organizations of deaf members opened during this time?

3. When did Captioned Films for the Deaf receive federal support?

4. Which president of the U.S. signed the bill establishing Caption Films for the Deaf?

5. Do you think many positive changes for deaf people took place from 1940–1960? Explain your answer.

Chapter 6   Jr. National Association of the Deaf

Pages 35–36

Comprehension Questions

1. Who suggested that the NAD establish a youth organization? When?

2. Who was the first director of the Jr. NAD?

3. Who succeeded Garretson and in what year?

4. Which director of the Jr. NAD served the organization longest?

5. Why was the Jr. NAD developed?

6. What are the major goals of the Jr. NAD?

7. What kinds of awards are given by the Jr. NAD?

8. What is *The Junior Deaf American?*

More About the Jr. NAD

Pages 36–37

Comprehension Questions

1. List three different conferences or conventions that have been held by Jr. NAD.

2. Where was the first national convention, and where was the most recent convention?

3. How many years has the Jr. NAD Youth Leadership Camp been held in Minnesota?

4. Why is Melinda Padden a good example for deaf youth today?

Follow-up Activities for Students

1. Trace the history of your own school's Jr. NAD group.
2. If there is no Jr. NAD chapter at your school, you may want to try to start one. Contact the NAD to find out the most recent Jr. NAD Director's name for information.
3. Have any students from your school attended a Jr. NAD Convention, Conference, or Youth Leadership Camp? If so, interview these students to find out more about their experiences.
4. Students should have access to *The Junior Deaf American* if there is a school Jr. NAD chapter. A good class project would be to submit an article for publication in the magazine.
5. For more information about the Jr. NAD write to: The Jr. NAD, 814 Thayer Avenue, Silver Spring, MD 20910

The Telephone Arrives

Page 37

Comprehension Questions

1. Who is the person responsible for making telephones accessible to deaf people?

2. What did Robert Weitbrecht invent that helped deaf people?

3. Why were telephones a hindrance to deaf people before the acoustic coupler was invented?

4. How have TDDs helped deaf people?

5. Have TDD machines improved over the years? How?

Follow-Up Activities for Students

1. A classroom demonstration of TDD usage and care should be given.
2. In states where TDDs are available on loan or free of charge to deaf people, students should be given application information.
3. The TDD Directory should be available for class referral with special note of emergency numbers.
4. Students may wish to receive a demonstration of various new TDDs by the local distributor. For more information about purchasing TDDs, consult the TDD Directory.
5. Class should work on TDD "etiquette."

Registry of the Interpreters for the Deaf

Pages 37–38

Comprehension Questions

1. What is the RID?

2. What did deaf people do to communicate with hearing doctors or lawyers before the interpreting profession was organized?

3. Did deaf people have well trained interpreters before the 1960s?

4. What is RID Certification?

5. How can a person become certified as an interpreter?

Follow-Up Activities for Students

1. If possible, a deaf person who has certification as a reverse skills (RSC) interpreter and a CSC hearing interpreter should visit the class and explain the roles of interpreters and their use.
2. Class can role play various interpreting situations with:
   a. interpreter breaking Code of Ethics.
   b. deaf person asking the interpreter questions.
   c. interpreter being used correctly.
3. Representative from local interpreter referral-agency should visit class and explain ways to request an interpreter.

Cued Speech

Pages 38–39

Comprehension Questions

1. Who developed "Cued Speech"?

2. During which decade did Cued Speech begin?

3. What are cues and why are they used?

4. Are cues like signs?

The Council of Organizations Serving the Deaf

Page 39

Comprehension Questions

1. What do the initials COSD represent?

2. When and where was COSD established?

3. Why was COSD founded?

4. Who provided COSD with a grant that allowed it to accomplish many things?

5. What role did Mervin Garretson have in COSD?

6. Is COSD still alive today? Why or why not?

Deaf Administrators

Pages 39–40

Comprehension Questions

1. When did the number of deaf administrators increase?

2. Name four deaf people who held positions of responsibility in the 1960s. What were their jobs?

3. If those early administrators had not succeeded, would there be many deaf administrators today? Why or why not?

The National Theatre of the Deaf

Pages 40–41

Comprehension Questions

1. Who submitted the *first* proposal to establish a theatre of the deaf? Was it approved?

2. When Hays and Bragg received their funding from the Department of Health, Education, and Welfare, what did they do with the money?

3. Has the National Theatre of the Deaf been successful? How do you know?

4. In Bernard Bragg's statement, he looked back on people's reactions to his use of sign language. Explain his statement in the last paragraph. Do you agree with his observations?

Time Line
1960–1969

Page 42

Comprehension Questions

1. How many *post-secondary* programs were opened to deaf students during this 10 year period?

2. Why do you think that services expanded during the 1960's?

3. Which new organizations serving deaf people were established during the 1960s?

4. On what project did the A.G. Bell Association and the NAD work together?

5. In what year did the National Theatre of the Deaf visit Europe?

Follow-Up Activities for Students

The sixties were a very important time for deaf people because of the rapid growth of human services. A class discussion of this trend would be appropriate. Talk about grant-in-aid funds available to college students seeking careers in human service. Why was so much money available during this era? How does it compare to the present time?

Additional Follow-Up

1. Students could be shown a film or videotape of the National Theatre of the Deaf. Discussion should follow focusing on the style of signs—what is artistic signing? Fairmont Theatre of the Deaf has filmed performances, and their style of signing is different. Gallaudet College also has videotapes called "Wanna Hear ASL Stories" which make an excellent comparison— conversational signing can be compared to NTD and Fairmont.
2. The publication *A Guide to College/Career Programs for Deaf Students* should be made available to high school students. The wide variety of post-secondary programs can be discussed and analyzed and compared to pre-'60s options.

Chapter 7 — Our Deaf World

Pages 43–46

Comprehension Questions

1. Why did Mr. Holcomb title his collection of anecdotes, "Hazards of Deafness"?

2. Do *you* think You Have To Be Deaf To Understand? Is there a special feeling that deaf people share? Describe the feeling.

3. Which of the authors were involved or are involved in deaf education? Where?

4. Some of the authors wrote funny stories and some more serious stories or poems. Which is your favorite and why?

Follow-Up Activities for Students

1. Write your own funny or serious poem about being deaf.
2. Compile a list of hazards common to your own experiences.
3. For further reading, the book by Holcomb could be made available to students.

Chapter 8   Periodicals for and by Deaf People

Pages 47–49

Comprehension Questions

1. Why is *The American Annals of the Deaf* famous?

2. What was the first periodical written *by* deaf people *for* deaf people?

3. Name five periodicals written by and for deaf people.

4. Why did *The Silent Worker* stop in 1929? When did it begin again and why?

5. Who was George S. Porter? What newspaper did he establish?

Follow-Up Activities for Students

1. Examine copies of: *The Silent News, The Broadcaster, The Deaf American, American Annals of the Deaf,* and any other available periodicals for deaf people.
2. Create a class newspaper that is either news or literary in nature.
3. Find out the history of your school newspaper if there is one.

The Buff and Blue

Page 49

Comprehension Questions

1. At what college is *The Buff and Blue* published?

2. Who writes the articles, stories, and poetry in *The Buff and Blue?*

3. Name five former editors of the Gallaudet College newspaper.

4. What literary work was the result of three people's "teamwork"?

5. For how many years has *The Buff and Blue* been published?

Follow-Up Activities for Students

1. Try to find copies of some of the publications mentioned above in your school library.
2. Contact Gallaudet College to order copies of *The Buff and Blue* for classroom use with this chapter.
3. Begin work on a class literary magazine.

Literary Efforts of Deaf Persons

Pages 49–50

Comprehension Questions

1. Who wrote *Legend of the Rock and Other Pieces?*

2. Which deaf person was the first to have his poetry published?

3. How many poems were in Nack's first book?

4. What was reported in *The Gallaudet Almanac* in 1974?

Published Deaf Authors

Comprehension Questions

1. Why is Howard L. Terry remembered today?

2. Name four published deaf authors.

3. Why did Terry receive an honorary degree from Gallaudet College?

Follow-Up Activities for Students

1. Use library catalogs to locate the work of the following authors: Leo Jacobs (*A Deaf Adult Speaks Out*); Thomas Spradley (*Deaf Like Me*); Joanne Greenberg (*In This Sign*).
2. After reading one of the above books, write a critique of it. Or, instead . . . teacher could obtain copies of each of the books and offer the students a synopsis of the stories to generate discussion.
3. Many activities can be developed by the teacher to stimulate student literary work such as Haiku poems, limericks, prose, autobiographies, etc.
4. Copies of the publication list of the NAD and Gallaudet College Bookstore can be used to demonstrate the wide variety of literature now being sold about deaf people, American Sign Language, the Deaf Community, and teaching deaf students.

Chapter 9   "The Noblest Gift"

Comprehension Questions

1. Why did George Veditz feel that sign language was noble?

2. Why did monks use signs?

3. How far back in history can we trace signs?

4. Who were Ponce de Leon and de l'Epee?

5. Why is American Sign Language a combination of French and American signs?

Follow-Up Activities for Students

1. Read and discuss the article "Everyone Here Spoke Sign Language" about the deaf and hearing community on Martha's Vineyard. Written by Nora Groce, it appeared in *The Deaf American*.
2. Compare signs you use with signs your parents (if deaf) or other deaf adults use, to see variations over time.

American Sign Language Comes Out of the Closet

Page 52

Comprehension Questions

1. Who was the chairman of the English Department of Gallaudet in the 1950s?

2. Why did Dr. Stokoe establish a research project?

3. What was the name of Dr. Stokoe's project?

4. Were any deaf people involved in Stokoe's research? How?

5. Stokoe published his conclusions in 1960. What are they?

6. How did other linguists react to Stokoe's publication?

The Continuing Work of Dr. William C. Stokoe, Jr.

Pages 52–53

Comprehension Questions

1. What is the name of the book written in honor of Dr. Stokoe?

2. When and where was this book given to Dr. Stokoe?

3. Who wrote the articles that were in the book given to Stokoe?

4. Who wrote *A Dictionary of American Sign Language on Linguistic Principles?*

5. Why is Dr. James Woodward remembered?

6. Is American Sign Language poor or sloppy English? Why or why not?

7. Some people have said ASL can not express abstract ideas. Is this true? Explain.

The Growth of Interest

Pages 53–54

Comprehension Questions

1. Has "Deaf Culture" always been accepted?

2. Is American Sign Language really broken English?

3. What is Carol Padden's profession?

4. Explain how the book honoring Stokoe is good for learning about Deaf Culture.

5. Who are T.J. O'Rourke, S. Melvin Carter, and Ella Mae Lentz? What do they have in common?

Follow-Up Activities for Students

1. Do biographical reports on:
   a. Dr. William Stokoe, Jr.
   b. Terrence J. O'Rourke
   c. S. Melvin Carter, Jr.
   d. Ella Mae Lentz
   e. Carol Padden
   f. Lou Fant
   g. Gilbert Eastman
   h. Bernard Bragg
   i. Charlotte Baker
   j. Barbara Kannapell
2. Do class presentations showing translations of English to American Sign Language, using written English for the former.
3. Write an original play using ASL, or study *Sign Me Alice* written by Gilbert Eastman.

4. Develop stories using:
   a. fingermime—using fingerspelling to illustrate the animal, person . . .
   b. signmime—using mime and sign to tell a vivid story.
   c. mime—using pantomime to tell a story.
5. Read books on Deaf Culture and ASL or see films. Examples of these are:
   a. *Sign Language and the Deaf Community*
   b. "Wanna See ASL Stories" (Gallaudet library)
   c. Simon Carmel's videotapes on Deaf Folklore from Gallaudet College.
6. If there are any deaf instructors of ASL at school, ask those teachers to speak to the class and teach basic grammatical structures of ASL and cultural anecdotes such as "Deaf Pah."
7. Discuss the concept of bilingualism—fluency in both languages, ASL and English.

Chapter 10   The Miss Deaf America Pageant

Page 55

Comprehension Questions

1. Name all of the Miss Deaf Americas since 1972.

2. Why did Pam Young replace Mary Pearce?

3. At what important convention did Mary Beth Barber win the pageant?

Follow-Up Activities for Students

1. Find out all of the names of Miss Deaf Pageant winners in your home state and interview one of these winners if possible.
2. Is there a Mr. Deaf State Pageant in your area? The same could apply.

Captioned Television

Pages 55–56

Comprehension Questions

1. Which man pioneered captioned television? Where did he work?

2. In what way was WGBH involved in early captioning?

3. What is a decoder?

The Caption Center at WGBH-TV

Pages 56–57

Comprehension Questions

1. When did WGBH begin captioning the ABC Evening News?

2. Describe the captioning process used to make the Captioned ABC News.

National Captioning Institute

Page 57

Comprehension Questions

1. What did the FCC do in 1976 which helped deaf people?

2. When the Sears, Roebuck Co. agreed to market the decoder, how did this help captioning grow?

3. Did any television networks show interest in captioning their shows? Which?

4. Is captioning a success?

Follow-Up Activities for Students

1. Class should have a demonstration of how a decoder works, including the text service which is now available.
2. Compare the way the news is captioned with the way a film on TV is captioned. A discussion of the pros and cons of "simultaneous captioning" should follow.
3. Do a research project about "teletext" and how it differs from Line 21 captioning.
4. A representative of the state association of the deaf could lecture the students about the 1981 demonstrations against CBS and their Line 21 policy. How did the NAD execute the demonstration? Was it successful?
5. The 1982 NAD Convention set a new priority to investigate and promote more access to television for deaf people. Interview people involved with the NAD to obtain more information about this new mandate.
6. Make a list of all captioned programs and the number of hours of captioning per week in their area.

Deaf Awareness Programs

Page 57

Comprehension Questions

1. When did Deaf Awareness activities begin? Why?

2. How did libraries become involved?

3. List two activities that were used to increase deaf awareness.

Follow-Up Activities for Students

1. Contact the state association of the deaf or local deaf clubs to find out if there are still Deaf Awareness activities going on. The class could attempt a similar activity in the school or community.
2. Develop a community activity to promote a positive image of deaf people (a car wash, bake sale, poster campaign, etc.).

Hearing Ear Dogs

Pages 57–58

Comprehension Questions

1. What year did the six dogs go to their deaf owners?

2. How did the program training Hearing Ear Dogs begin?

3. What kinds of jobs do these specially trained dogs do?

4. Where could you write for more information about Hearing Ear Dogs?

Follow-Up Activities for Students

1. Contact the Humane Association to get information about or a demonstration of their Hearing Ear Dog program. Any student who has a Hearing Ear Dog could tell about the program or show how the dog helps him or her.

Public Law 94-142

Page 58

Comprehension Questions

1. When was PL 94-142 signed and by whom?

2. In what way are parents included in the law?

3. How has PL 94-142 affected deaf students?

4. What is mainstreaming?

5. Do you attend a mainstreamed or all-deaf program? How do you feel about this issue—should deaf children be in classes with hearing students? Why or why not?

6. Have your parents attended IEP meetings? Were you there too?

Follow-Up Activities for Students

1. The teacher should show *all* students *their* IEP's so that they can see their own educational plan. A discussion of goals may or may not follow.
2. Class should debate self-containment of deaf students versus mainstreaming. Each side should be required to research its topic carefully.

Deaf Ph.D.'s

Pages 58–59

Comprehension Questions

1. What is a Ph.D.?

2. Have any deaf people earned Ph.D's?

3. What is James Marster's occupation?

4. Can deaf people work as doctors and dentists? Explain how you know this.

Follow-Up Activities for Students

1. Refer to pp. 439–442 in *Deaf Heritage* to see the partial list of deaf people who have earned doctorates.
2. Contact local universities to find out whether any deaf people have earned doctoral degrees there.

The White House Conference

Page 59

Comprehension Questions

1. What was the purpose of the White House Conference on Handicapped Individuals?

2. How many Americans were disabled in 1977?

3. How many disabled people attended the conference?

4. What percentage of the delegates were hearing impaired?

5. What was Don Pettingill's function during the conference?

6. What could the conference recommendations do to help disabled people?

7. How did President Carter show he wanted to communicate with deaf people?

Chapter 11

The Ear: Outer and Middle

Pages 60–61

Comprehension Questions

1. In what way are animal and human pinnas different?

2. Look up the word "conductive" in the dictionary. Why do you think damage to the middle or outer ear area is called a "conductive" loss?

3. What are the names of the three bones in the middle ear?

4. Which of the ossicles is largest?

5. What are three causes of conductive losses?

The Ear: Inner

Pages 61–62

Comprehension Questions

1. What are the two structures of the inner ear?

2. Why do some deaf people also have problems with equilibrium?

3. Why is sensory-neural loss permanent?

4. What are cochlear implants?

5. As sound enters the ear, travels through the auditory canal and into the middle ear, it causes vibration. When the middle ear vibrates, it stimulates the inner ear. The inner ear fluid does not vibrate. It moves in waves and stimulates the hair cells. What happens after the hair cells are stimulated? Explain fully.

6. If a person had a perfect cochlea, a perfect auditory nerve, and a damaged brain, do you think they would still hear normally? Why or why not?

7. Label the following parts of the ear on the diagram below:
   a. pinna
   b. auditory canal
   c. eardrum
   d. malleus
   e. incus
   f. stapes
   g. semi-circular canals
   h. cochlea
   i. auditory nerve

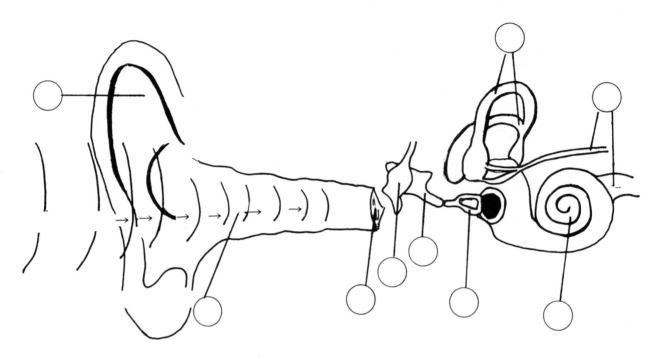

Follow-Up Activities for Students

1. Do further reading on:
   a. cochlear implant research
   b. otosclerosis and surgery to correct it (stapedectomy)
   c. the physics of sound (the four transformations of sound as it travels through the ear)
   d. hearing aid developments and/or history
2. A class model of the ear should be used for students to manipulate.
3. An audiologist should be invited to the class to explain more about hearing aids and their functions and limitations.

Causes of Hearing Loss: Prenatal and In Infancy

Pages 62–64

Comprehension Questions

1. What is rubella?

2. How can genes cause deafness?

3. Do many deaf parents have deaf babies?

4. What is Waardenburg's Syndrome?

5. How can you tell if someone has Usher's Syndrome?

6. What are three causes of deafness in infants?

7. What is a forceps delivery? How can it cause deafness?

8. List three prelingual causes of deafness.

9. Do you think it would be easier for a child to go to school if he or she were prelingually deaf or postlingually deaf? Why?

10. Are you prelingually deaf? Why are you deaf?

11. Do you know any postlingual causes of deafness? What are they?

Follow-Up Activities for Students

1. Do an independent project on the etiology of your own deafness. If it is unknown, students could pick an etiology to research.
2. Discuss postlingual causes for deafness. Included in the discussion should be childhood diseases such as mumps and ear infections, accidents, illnesses such as meningitis and fevers, and the effects of medications.

3. Conduct a survey of the deaf student population to determine the most common etiologies (causes) of deafness. (See Questionnaire that follows.)
4. Invite visitors to speak to the class about their own deafness. Suggested are:
   a. a deaf person who has Waardenburg's Syndrome.
   b. a person with Usher's Syndrome using tactile communication.
   c. deaf parents of deaf children.
   d. a person who has meningitis-caused deafness (i.e. balance problems at night).
   e. postlingually deaf person talking about shock of losing hearing.
   f. a person who has Klippel-Feil Syndrome, to talk about this genetic syndrome and its ramifications.
5. Research a genetic syndrome and present it to the class. Suggested are:
   a. Waardenburg's Syndrome.
   b. Alports' Syndrome.
   c. Down's Syndrome.
   d. Klippel-Feil Syndrome.

Follow-Up Activity Questionnaire

Interview as many students as possible in your school or program. Based on the information recorded on this chart, the class should come up with a profile of the causes (etiologies) of deafness. Which was most common? Which students are multi-handicapped and why?

D.O.B. _____
(date of birth)

NAME _____

Check 1:
____ a. RUBELLA
____ b. BLOOD INCOMPATIBILITY
____ c. GENETIC
____ d. FORCEPS DELIVERY
____ e. PREMATURE

____ f. MENINGITIS
____ g. EAR INFECTION
____ h. ACCIDENT
____ i. FEVER
____ j. UNKNOWN

Check 1 or more:
____ ALL HEARING FAMILY
____ DEAF PARENTS
____ DEAF SIBLINGS
____ DEAF RELATIVES
____ (grandparent,
____ cousins,
____ aunts-uncles)

Chapter 12   The World of Sports

Pages 65–66

Comprehension Questions

1. Although the team "died" in 1925, did the Goodyear Silents have a strong record?

2. Have any deaf people played professional sports? What sport?

3. What was the original name for the World Games for the Deaf?

4. When did the U.S. send its first athletes to the international competition?

5. What is the AAAD?

6. What are the 6 goals of the AAAD?

Follow-Up Activities for Students

1. Do research on the following deaf athletes:
   a. Paul D. Hubbard (football)
   b. William Hoy (baseball)
   c. LeRoy Colombo (swimming)
   d. Eugene Hairston (boxing)
   e. Lou Ferrigno (body building)
   f. Kitty O'Neil (racing and diving)
   g. S. Robey Burns (organizing American participation in Games)
   h. Art Kruger ("Father of AAAD")
2. Contact a local deaf club to find out the schedule for its athletic competitions. Students may attend or join a team if they are eligible.
3. Refer to *Deaf Heritage* pp. 311–315. The charts of records held by various teams and individual players should be of interest. Students may recognize the names of some or even find their own school among the record holders!

Chapter 13 Years 1880–1920

Pages 67–68

Comprehension Questions

1. How many people participated in the first convention of the NAD?

2. How many participated in the convention 30 years later?

3. Was there an increase or decrease in membership between 1880 and 1920? How many people attended in 1920?

4. What types of issues concerned the NAD?

5. Were women allowed to participate in NAD elections? How do you know?

6. What did the NAD do to help deaf Americans?

Years 1921–1960

Pages 68–69

Comprehension Questions

1. Although automobiles helped many people travel more, deaf people were penalized. Explain.

2. How did the NAD help the U.S. during World War II?

3. What types of legal cases involved deaf people between 1920–1960?

4. Who were William Hoy and Luther Taylor?

5. What was happening in Iowa in 1960 that upset deaf people?

Years 1961–1980

Pages 70–71

Comprehension Questions

1. The NAD bought a large building in Silver Spring, Maryland, in 1971. Several other organizations for the deaf have offices there now. What is the name of the building purchased in 1971?

2. When Frederick Schreiber died, who succeeded him as executive director of the NAD?

3. What are the names of the NAD's publications?

4. What cities hosted NAD conventions between 1960–1980?

5. In the past, the NAD has tried to improve services for the deaf. Recently, the NAD has become involved in captioning television. What other areas do *you* feel the NAD should improve?

Follow-Up Activities for Students

1. Research the Amy Rowley legal case and investigate the involvement of the NAD Legal Defense Fund.
   a. Who is Amy Rowley and why did her parents go to court?
   b. How was the NAD involved in the case?
   c. What were the results of the court case?
   d. How do students *feel* about the results?
2. In 1983, the NAD sponsored a mass demonstration against CBS Television because that network had refused to provide Line-21 captions. Research what CBS-TVs position is regarding captioned television now. The class could follow-up this research with a debate: Is (or was) CBS violating the rights of deaf people?
3. The NAD has continued to be interested in education of deaf people. Read recent issues of *The Deaf American* and *The Broadcaster* and try to find examples of the NAD's political involvement in education.
4. Refer to the list of NAD presidents and select one or more to research. Numerous books are in print that offer biographical information on many deaf leaders.
5. If your school is located in the Central Atlantic area, a field trip can be organized to visit Halex House, home of the National Association of the Deaf, Captioned Films for the Deaf, Junior National Association of the Deaf, Registry of Interpreters for the Deaf, and other organizations.